Swampland Flowers

Swampland Flowers

The Letters and Lectures
of Zen Master Ta Hui

Translated by J. C. Cleary

Shambhala
Boston & London
2006

Shambhala Publications, Inc.
4720 Walnut Street
Boulder, Colorado 80301
www.shambhala.com

Printed in the United States of America
Designed by Margery Cantor

∞ This edition is printed on acid-free paper that meets
the American National Standards Institute Z39.48 Standard.
♻ Shambhala Publications makes every effort to print on recycled paper.
For more information please visit www.shambhala.com.
Shambhala Publications is distributed worldwide by Penguin
Random House, Inc., and its subsidiaries.

Library of Congress Cataloging-in-Publication Data
Zonggao, 1089–1163.
[Zhi yue lu. 31–32. English. Selections.]
Swampland flowers: the letters and lectures of Zen master Ta hui [i.e. Zonggao] /
translated by J. C. Cleary.—1st Shambhala ed.
p. cm.
Translation of selection of juan 31 and 32 of Zhi yue lu.
ISBN 978-1-64547-083-0 (pbk.: alk paper)
1. Zen Buddhism—Doctrines—Early works to 1800.   2. Zonggao,
1089–1163—Correspondence—Early works to 1800.   3. Priests, Zen—China—
Correspondence—Early works to 1800.   I. Cleary, J. C. (Jonathan Christopher)

BQ9268.Z65213   2006
294.3'927'092—dc22
2005051813

Contents

Preface

This book gives a translation of some letters and lectures on Ch'an by the great teacher Ta Hui. His remarks translated from Chinese here were in the main addressed to people in lay life, so the emphasis is on ways by which people immersed in worldly doings can learn Ch'an and achieve the liberation promised by Buddha. Though more than eight hundred years have passed since Ta Hui lived, the gist of his message is not bound to any particular time, place, or mode of expression— hopefully his words will still hit home and help people of today to unfold their potential.

About the Author

Ta Hui was born into the cosmopolitan world of the Sung dynasty. It was an age when both rationalistic philosophy and practical invention flourished, when printed books multiplied and the arts reached a mature sophistication still admired today. Communication and commerce intensified: five Chinese cities had populations over a million. Talents from all over the country were drawn to the brilliant circles in the imperial capital.

This was no charmed golden age, unself-conscious and unquestioning. The political sensibilities of many upper-class Chinese were affronted by the relative weakness of the dynasty towards the powerful "barbarian" states pressing in on the northeast and northwest, and reform measures to strengthen the government and augment its revenue were great issues of controversy among gentlemen of affairs. The productive classes felt the pressure directly, as it was they who had to finance the swollen, ineffective army, and the heavy payments of silver and silk sent as tribute to the enemy. Pressure of taxation undercut the position of the small producers, more and more of whom had to give up their independence for the patronage of a big landlord who could fend off the tax burden through political pull. As the government tried to increase its revenue, it succeeded more in driving the nation's wealth beyond its own reach into powerful private hands, while millions of little people were deprived of their livelihood altogether.

Finally in the 1120s the dam broke. In 1126 the forces of the "barbarian" Chin state to the northeast captured the capital, Pien, along with the reigning emperor, his retired father, and a large number of high officials and top courtiers. Soon the Chin had set up their own puppets over vast stretches of China north of the Yangtse, and even the cities of south China were not immune from their raids. The Sung government regrouped around a new emperor and a new capital in the south, and eventually settled on a policy of acquiescence to Chin rule over north China. The old capital of the Northern Sung became the capital of the Chin (Pien, the modern K'aifeng, just south of the Yellow River) while the Southern Sung ruled from Lin An (the modern Hangchou, in Chekiang).

Ch'an Buddhism by Sung times was outwardly flourishing: it had arrived culturally and socially. The impact of Ch'an teaching and style had been felt up to the highest level of society, and many highly placed gentlemen of affairs considered themselves adherents. When Ta Hui lived some four hundred years had passed since the early greats of Ch'an's florescence had "opened mountains," clearing land in remote spots with their followers to farm for their livelihood. Now there were large official establishments, with revenues assigned by the state. Recognized adepts could be summoned by imperial "invitation" to take up residence and teach at these centers. Control over the possessions and capital of these places could become the object of conflicting desires and power struggles: established Buddhism was certainly not free of the taint of worldly ambition. Ta Hui's teacher Yuan Wu often exclaimed how numerous phony Ch'an followers had become.

Ta Hui was born in 1088 in Hsuan Ch'eng, just south of the Yangtse River in Anwhei, a son of the Hsi family. At school he soon showed a preference for Buddhism over worldly studies.

Even at an early age he was considered remarkable throughout the vicinity. At the age of sixteen he left home; at seventeen, he "dropped his hair," having his head shaved as a monk.

He took delight in the doings of the Ch'an school, and read through the records of all the houses (the "Five Houses" named for classic masters of Ch'an: Kuei-Yang, Lin Chi, Ts'ao-Tung, Yun Men, and Fa Yen). He especially liked the words of Yun Men and (his teacher) Mu Chou. But he had doubts about the five sects: since originally there had been but one Bodhidharma, why were there so many schools? By nature he was exceptionally talented and not bound by convention.

At nineteen Ta Hui began his travels, following the traditional practice in Ch'an of visiting the various communities and seeking instruction from the teachers there. Even at this early age, Ta Hui would be taken for a later embodiment of previous Ch'an Masters. From one he sought instruction on Hsueh Tou's hundred verses eulogizing the ancients (Hsueh Tou's verse comments on one hundred well-known public cases of Ch'an, which became the kernel of the *Blue Cliff Record* of Ta Hui's teacher, Yuan Wu). The teacher would not offer a word of explanation, but made Ta Hui express his own view: in every case Ta Hui completely comprehended the subtle meaning. The older master exclaimed, "You must be someone who's come again!"

From long contact with the Ts'ao-Tung tradition communities, Ta Hui understood their message thoroughly, but he saw the formalized, ceremonious way they certified the transmission, and repudiated it, thinking to himself, "If there were transmission in Ch'an, how could this be the self-realized, self-awakened-to Dharma of the ancestral teachers?"

Later he was directed to go to Master Chun of Chan T'ang. When Ta Hui first got there his intellectualism was unrestrained. One day Chan T'ang asked, "Why are your nostrils boundless today?" Ta Hui replied, "(Because) I'm at your place." T'ang said, "You phony Ch'an man."

Again, when Ta Hui was reading a scripture, Chan T'ang asked, "What scripture are you reading?" He answered, "The Diamond Sutra." T'ang said, " 'This Dharma is everywhere equal, without high or low.' Why is Yun Chu Mountain high and Pao Feng Mountain low?" Ta Hui replied, " 'This Dharma is everywhere equal, without high or low.' " T'ang said, "You could be a lecturer's assistant."

One day Chan T'ang said, "Reverend Kao (Ta Hui's initiatory name was Tsung Kao), you understood my Ch'an here at once. When I had you explain, you could explain, and when I had you give informal talks or general lectures commenting on and extolling the ancients, you could do that too. There's just one thing that's not there: do you know what?" Ta Hui answered, "What?" T'ang said, "You only lack this one liberation that's in the burst of power. If you don't get this one liberation, there's Ch'an while I'm talking with you in private, but as soon as you leave the private room, there's not; there's Ch'an while you're awake and thinking, but as soon as you fall asleep, there's not. If you're like this, how can you be a match for birth and death?" Ta Hui replied, "This is precisely my point of doubt."

When Chan T'ang was extremely ill, Ta Hui asked him, "If you don't recover, whom should I take as a teacher so I can complete this great affair?" T'ang said, "There's a fellow from Szechuan named Ch'in (Yuan Wu's initiatory name was K'e Ch'in). Though I don't know him, you must place your reliance in him, and you'll be able to complete your affair. If you see him without completely comprehending, then go on practicing, and in a later life you'll appear and learn Ch'an."

When Ta Hui met him, Yuan Wu was staying at T'ien Ning Monastery (in the imperial capital, Pien). On his way there Ta Hui said to himself, "I'll make nine summers the time limit: if his Ch'an is no different from the other places, and he falsely considers himself right, then I'll write that there is no Ch'an. A great scripture or treatise is better than wasting energy and getting bogged down for years. By cultivating the fundamentals, I'll not slip from being a man of the Buddha Dharma in future lives." When he got to see Yuan Wu, he was asking for instruction all day long.

Yuan Wu brought up Yun Men's saying, "East Mountain walks on the water," and had Ta Hui come to grips with it. Ta Hui offered some forty-nine replies but Yuan Wu didn't approve. One day Yuan Wu had gone up to his seat (to teach the assembly), and he cited Yun Men's words and said, "I am not this way. If someone asks, 'What is the place where all the buddhas appear?' I just say to them, 'From the south comes a fragrant wind, producing a slight chill in the recesses of the palace.'" Hearing this, Ta Hui emptied out, and thought he was enlightened. Yuan Wu investigated and found that though Ta Hui had managed to get before and after cut off, so the aspect of motion does not arise, yet he was settling down in purity and nakedness. He told Ta Hui, "It wasn't easy for you to get to this stage—too bad that having died, you are unable to come back to life. Without a doubt, words and phrases are a great disease, but haven't you seen the saying

Hanging from a cliff, let go—
And agree to accept the experience.
After annihilation, come back to life—
I couldn't deceive you.

You must be aware that this truth exists." Ta Hui said, "Just based on today's attainment, I'm already joyous and lively; I can't understand any more."

Yuan Wu directed Ta Hui to spend time receiving and conversing with gentlemen of affairs who came calling. Whenever Ta Hui entered his room for private instruction, Yuan Wu brought up the same saying every time: "Having words or wordlessness, both are like clinging vines on the tree." Questioning him with this, Yuan Wu would immediately say "Wrong, that's not it!" as soon as Ta Hui opened his mouth. Ta Hui said, "This truth is like a dog looking at a pan of hot oil, wanting to taste it but unable to, wanting to give it up but unable to." Yuan Wu said, "You've described it very well—this is the unbreakable trap, the thicket of thorns."

One day Ta Hui said, "I hear that when you were at Wu Tsu's you asked about this saying. I wonder what Wu Tsu said." Yuan Wu laughed but did not answer. Ta Hui said, "At the time you must have asked in front of the assembly: what's stopping you from saying it now?" Yuan Wu said, "I asked the meaning of 'Having words or wordlessness, both are like clinging vines on the tree.' Wu Tsu said, 'Describe it and it can't be described completely, depict it and it can't be depicted accurately.' I also asked, 'How is it when the tree falls and the vines wither?' Wu Tsu said, 'It comes along with it.'" At these words, Ta Hui was released, saying, "I understand." So then Yuan Wu brought up several particularly difficult cases in order to question Ta Hui, who replied to them all without getting stuck. Yuan Wu said, "At last I know I haven't been deceiving you." After this Yuan Wu accepted him as the heir to the true school of Lin Chi.

After his great penetration, Ta Hiu went back to several figures in Ch'an he had doubts about and asked Yuan Wu about them. Yuan Wu said, "My Ch'an here is like a great ocean: to get it right, you have to take a great ocean and pour it in. If you just take a bowl, fill it with a little, and stop there, it's that your capacity is only like this—what would you have me do about it? Only a few can reach your level. There was one equal to you (among my students), but he has already died."

Before long Yuan Wu had divided the teaching duties with

Ta Hui (showing that Yuan Wu considered his attainment full enough for Ta Hui to be fit to guide others). Soon Ta Hui was widely esteemed throughout the Ch'an communities. He came to the notice of a high minister and was given a purple robe and the name "Buddha Sun" as a sign of imperial honor.

When the Chin forces took the Sung capital in 1126, Ta Hui was well enough known to be on their list; he had to flee south to avoid being part of the booty. The new emperor Kao Tsung "invited" Yuan Wu to take up residence at Yun Chu Monastery (just west of Nan Ch'ang City in Kiangsi). Ta Hui himself went there, and Yuan Wu invited him to be the head monk. Once a Ch'an Master came forth from the assembly and asked, "How is it when the sword is hanging (right over you pointed) right between your eyes?" Ta Hui said, "The blood squirts up to heaven." From below the (teacher's) seat, Yuan Wu held him back with his hand saying, "Stop! stop! Well asked, even more amazingly answered."

Whenever Ta Hui entered Yuan Wu's teaching room, Yuan Wu would always listen to his words. Afterwards one day, as they were going to their private quarters, Yuan Wu said, "If there were a Ch'an man like me, how would you deal with him?" Ta Hui said, "What unexpected good fortune if there were! As Tung P'o said, having been an executioner all my life, when I meet a fat fellow, I slice." Yuan Wu laughed loudly and said, "Rather it's you who should enter the room with me (and be my teacher)—you've pinned me to the wall." (By tradition in Ch'an only those who surpassed their teachers were really worthy heirs.)

Yuan Wu also asked Ta Hui how he'd transmit Bodhidharma's coming from the West. Ta Hui said, "I shouldn't always be making up wild fox spirit views." (A "wild fox spirit" is a metaphor for someone with unrestrained freedom of action, but it also carries a negative sense of one who indulges in cleverness.)

Yuan Wu also asked, "Sitting on the tiger's head, gathering in the tiger's tail, understanding the source meaning at the first phrase—what is the first (highest, supreme) phrase?" Ta Hui said, "This is the second phrase."

Yuan Wu often said that in recent times Ch'an had become just a cliché, a nest, for most of the people in the various communities of seekers. But Ta Hui he deeply approved, and considered him the lone worthy successor to the lineage coming through Yuan Wu's teacher, Wu Tsu Fa Yen.

When Yuan Wu returned to his native Szechuan, Ta Hui stayed on, building himself a hut behind Yun Chu Mountain. Students flocked to him. Later he transferred his teaching activities to the southeast, to Fukien. In 1137 he received an imperial summons to dwell in a Ch'an temple on Ching Shan Mountain, near the new imperial capital Lin An (Hangchou). Within a year over a thousand disciples had gathered, and Ta Hui was becoming known as the great reviver of Lin Chi Ch'an. Another year, and the congregation surpassed seventeen hundred.

High circles in the government were rent with dissension over whether to go on the offensive against the Chin and try to reconquer northern China, or to be content with consolidating their southern domain. Repercussions of this political struggle reached Ta Hui when a high courtier with whom he was acquainted ran afoul of the prime minister for opposing his capitulationist policies, so that he and all his supposed supporters were sent into exile. Ta Hui was stripped of his imperial honors and certification, and ordered away from the capital to the backcountry of southeast Hunan and then to a malarial area in Kuangtung. Of course he continued the teaching of Ch'an, and in one summer is said to have produced thirteen enlightened people. A son of the royal house who was king over the area was greatly impressed when he happened to hear Ta Hui lecture. This man arranged for Ta Hui to be exonerated: at the age of sixty-eight, after fifteen years away, he returned to the heart of the empire. He was first assigned to a temple east of the capital, and then back to Ching Shan. He requested to be excused from official temple duties, and in 1161 he was allowed to retire to the "Bright Moon Hall" at Ching Shan.

When his old acquaintance ascended the throne in 1163 as Emperor Hsiao Tsung, Ta Hui came under imperial protection. It was this emperor who bestowed the title "Ch'an Master of Great Wisdom" from which the name Ta Hui comes, and who caused Ta Hui's words to be included in the Great Canon a few years after his death.

It was 1163, on the ninth day of the eighth month, after showing signs of illness, when Ta Hui told the congregation of monks, nuns, and laypeople, "Tomorrow I'm going." Towards the predawn hours, after he'd written his last bequest and a letter to the emperor, the monk who was his attendant asked Ta Hui for a verse. In a serious voice Ta Hui said, "Without a verse, I couldn't die." He took up the brush and wrote:

Birth is thus
Death is thus
Verse or no verse
What's the fuss?

Then he let go of the writing brush and passed on. He had lived seventy-five years, fifty-eight in Ch'an. Records of his teachings were assembled by his disciples.

Acknowledgment

I could never have read Ta Hui's words, or undertaken to translate them, without the encouragement and guidance of my brother, Thomas Cleary.

Translator's Introduction

Drawing his concepts and images from the Buddhist Treasury, Ta Hui taught people for whom these were familiar ideas with definite associations. Translating his words for a time and place where Buddhism is not so widely known calls for an introduction to some indispensable terms whose foreign names and unfamiliar meaning might otherwise be unknown. Those familiar with the outlook of Mahayana Buddhism, those who already know the meanings of words like Buddha, Dharma, Bodhisattva, and Tathagata, can proceed directly to Ta Hui's letters. This discussion of background assumptions as well as the footnotes in the text on more specific points, are based on the great panopticon of Buddhist teachings, the *Tsung Ching Lu*, composed by the tenth century Chinese Buddhist adept known as Yen Shou.

Buddha taught beings according to their kind with methods and doctrines suited to their needs and abilities. Therefore there is no fixed doctrine, only various expedient teachings. At different levels of the teaching, the same words are used with different connotations, in different contrasts. It is acknowledged that this great affair of becoming enlightened cannot be conveyed fully in words, yet we cannot do without words either.

"Buddhism" is the Buddha Dharma, the teaching of the

enlightened one; often it's called simply "The Dharma," meaning "the Teaching" or "the Truth." Naturally the true teaching is one with reality itself: this idea is facilitated by the very word "dharma," which besides meaning "teaching, doctrine, method" also means "thing": physical objects and mental concepts, in fact all phenomena, are dharmas; the world of the dharmas is one with the world of The Dharma, the one reality.

Twenty-five hundred years ago this teaching appeared through the Indian sage Gautama, known as Shakyamuni Buddha, "The World-Honored One." In the face of suffering and death, worldly living lost its meaning and appeal for the hitherto sheltered young prince, who left his family and position to seek a way out of the cycle of birth and death. For six years he tried such methods of spiritual cultivation as were current in his day without finding liberation. At last, at age thirty-five, he achieved his own enlightenment, penetrating through to the extinction of desire, hatred, and ignorance, through to unconditioned reality, to nirvana. For him the things of the world were finished and done with, yet Shakyamuni rose from his seat of enlightenment to teach worldly beings. Devising all sorts of suitable teachings, unobstructed by worldly circumstances, he preached for forty-five years to all classes of the population, "Turning the Wheel of the Dharma."

Shakyamuni Buddha thus actualized to the highest degree the bodhisattva ideal. To be bodhisattvas, those who are enlightened must not grasp the experience, but rather be able to detach from detachment, freely to reenter the worlds of delusion to benefit the beings who make their homes there. Yen Shou says that, if there's only transcendental wisdom contemplating the real aspect (which is formless and changeless), without knowledge of the provisional involved with existence, this is being sunk down and stuck in emptiness. The Hua Yen Sutra says that bodhisattvas do not enter the world outside of emptiness, and do not enter emptiness outside of the world.

As it came down through time, the Buddhist Teaching has been elaborated in many schemes analyzing psychology and being. Shakyamuni found that the afflictions of worldly existence arise through a process of interdependent causation. Ignorance—volitional activity (creating karma)—consciousness—name and form—the senses (including conceptual mind as the sixth)—contact—sensation—desire—clinging—becoming—birth—old age, suffering, and death: all twelve links are present in each and every instant of deluded consciousness. What we perceive as external world and internal "I" are laboriously maintained delusions of false consciousness, "self-created, self-received." The inconstant, unsatisfying "reality" that traps us is our own doing, the product of force of habit, a fabrication, like a dream or magical illusion. So our acts (karma) determine our consciousness and being. Buddhism has seen a range of techniques evolved for breaking these bonds and awakening to the liberated essence.

Shakyamuni was a historical figure, the Buddha. But the word "buddha" is used in a wider sense too. First, other buddhas before and after Shakyamuni have appeared and will appear to make a mark on the world as great teachers. More generally, since all beings share in the same enlightened nature, all are (potential) buddhas: innately endowed with a formless, changeless, inherently awake real nature, we can reveal and master the use of it, and thus "become buddha." We all have a naturally real buddha "within"—an essence completely perceptive and aware that is also called the One Mind, and True Thusness.

Buddha often referred to himself and other buddhas as "tathagatas." Tathagata means "the one who has come from the truth," or "from the truth," as the Chinese explain their translation of it: "Tathagata means 'coming from within the self-nature of the one mind's true thusness.' 'Thusness' is changeless and invariant, and doesn't lose its own identity. True thusness not keeping to its own changeless void nature, but appearing according to circumstances, is the 'coming.' Actually, this is coming without coming." (Yen Shou)

The embryo of a tathagata is there in all sentient beings; this is the same as saying that everyone has buddha-nature. People who mistake their self-centered perceptions for reality, and accept their stock of habits as all there is, completely miss their true nature in their folly. In that delusion may be said to hide this ever-present reality, the world of sentient beings can be called the womb of the tathagatas, the repository of thusness. When revealed, so that without being removed phenomena don't obstruct truth and form doesn't defile emptiness, it's called Buddha's body of reality, the Dharmakaya. "The oneness of the universe is the everywhere-equal body of reality." The Hua Yen Sutra says: "Buddha's body fills the universe, appearing everywhere before all sentient beings, proceeding to effect according to causes—there's nowhere it doesn't extend to while always upon this seat of enlightenment."

The Ch'an adepts of China considered themselves heirs of a direct mind-to-mind transmission reaching from Shakyamuni Buddha himself through a succession of twenty-eight ancestral teachers in India to Bodhidharma, who brought Ch'an to China around the late fifth or early sixth century and became its First Ancestral Teacher there. Bodhidharma, it is said, "directly pointed to people's minds, letting them see their inherent nature and become buddha." Ch'an is a separate transmission outside of verbal doctrines, but by no means opposed to the Buddhist scriptures (sutras), which Ta Hui and other Ch'an men refer to as "The Teachings" when they quote from them. The Sanskrit names you'll encounter are figures from the scriptures: Maitreya, the future buddha; Manjusri, the bodhisattva who represents wisdom; Indra, the lord of heaven; Sudhana, Shariputra, and Subhuti, disciples of the Buddha.

Frequently Ta Hui quotes Vimalakirti, the hero of a sutra who exemplifies an enlightened being of vast spiritual powers who yet lives in the world as a householder.

By Ta Hui's time tales of the sayings and doings of the early classic figures of Chinese Ch'an were employed as teaching material. Well-known stories and sayings became "public cases" to come to grips with in meditation, and were used as problems to test the realization of students. Those with Chinese names Ta Hui mentions or quotes are mainly great adepts of the preceding four centuries of Ch'an in China. Perhaps most often cited is Yung Chia, who spent one day with the Sixth Ancestral Teacher and received his approval. Biographies of many of these famous masters can be found appended to the *Blue Cliff Record.*

Buddhism keeps in view the fact that even good things such as its liberative techniques and spiritual guides can become obstacles to the Path when they are objects of attachment. It's all right to use a method to enter the Path, but if you stick to it as the ultimate it becomes a sickness. Seeing his contemporaries indulging in verbalism with the "public cases," memorizing the "right answers," Ta Hui went so far as to stop the circulation of his teacher's great work of commentary on them, the *Blue Cliff Record.* Likewise, he struggled against the infatuation with quiet meditation that was prevalent in his time under the rubric of "silent illumination." Of course Ta Hui was not at odds with the living essence of the Ts'ao-Tung tradition: the great reviver of Ts'ao-Tung Ch'an who was his contemporary, Hung Chih, left Ta Hui in charge of his affairs when he died. So we must recognize that not only do those who cling to and intellectualize the techniques of meditation go astray, but that, even correctly applied, no technique is the answer for all time: they're all just temporary gates.

This translation is based on the Chinese text found in the

Chih Yueh Lu (Records of Pointing at the Moon), volumes thirty-one and thirty-two. Some of this material has been deleted where it seemed to require too much familiarity with many "public cases." What appears below represents the bulk of the Chinese text. The letters are arranged in the same order as in the original, with headings for each item provided by the translator. Where an elliptical Chinese phrase conveys information or associations familiar enough to Ta Hui's audience to be unstated, but which are not apparent to modern readers, the translator has filled out the meaning with parenthetical additions in the text, e.g., "Not until the (nonexistent) Year of the Ass." Given the lack of full, precise, one-to-one equivalencies from language to language, the translator has chosen to vary the rendition of phrases, formulas, and sayings that keep cropping up, in order to indicate more fully the range of meaning. Every effort has been made to insure the continuous flow of the English text, to convey something of the direct and forceful eloquence of Ta Hui's teaching style.

Swampland Flowers

To Li Hsien-ch'en

1 Clear the Mind

Buddha said, if you want to know the realm of buddhahood, you must make your mind as clear as empty space and leave false thinking and all grasping far behind, causing your mind to be unobstructed wherever it may turn. The realm of buddhahood is not some external world where there is a formal "Buddha": it's the realm of the wisdom of a self-awakened sage.

Once you are determined that you want to know this realm, you do not need adornment, cultivation, or realization to attain it. You must clear away the stains of afflictions from alien sensations that have been on your mind since beginningless time, (so that your mind) is as broad and open as empty space, detached from all the clinging of the discriminating intellect, and your false, unreal, vain thoughts too are like empty space. Then this wondrous effortless mind will be unimpeded wherever it goes.

2 Mindlessness

An ancient worthy had a saying: "To look for the ox, one must seek out its tracks. To study the Path, seek out Mindlessness. Where the tracks are, so must the ox be." The path of Mindlessness is easy to seek out. So-called "Mindlessness" is not being inert and unknowing like earth, wood, tile, or stone; it means that the mind is settled and imperturbable when in contact with situations and meeting circumstances; that it does not cling to anything, but is clear in all places, without hindrance or obstruction; without being stained, yet without dwelling in the stainlessness; viewing body and mind like dreams or illusions, yet without remaining in the perspective of dreams' and illusions' empty nothingness. Only when one arrives at a realm like this can it be called true Mindlessness. No, it's not lip-service mindlessness: if you haven't attained true Mindlessness and just go by the verbal kind, how is this different from the perverted Ch'an of "silent illumination"?*

"Just get to the root, don't worry about the branches." Emptying this mind is the root. Once you get the root, the fundamental, then all kinds of language and knowledge and all your daily activities as you respond to people and adapt to circumstances, through so many upsets and downfalls, whether joyous or angry, good or bad, favorable or adverse—these are all trivial matters, the branches. If you can be spontaneously aware and knowing as you are going along with circumstances, then there is neither lack nor excess.

---

* Ta Hui uses "silent illumination" in a pejorative way to criticize those who emphasized stillness and quiescence in themselves as the ultimate, without making empowerment through enlightenment the standard.

3 **Tend the Ox**

Since you're studying this Path, then at all times, in your en-
counters with people and responses to circumstances, you
must not let wrong thoughts continue. If you cannot see
through them, then the moment a wrong thought comes up
you should quickly concentrate your mental energy to pull
yourself away. If you always follow those thoughts and let
them continue without a break, not only does this obstruct the
Path, but it makes you out to be a man without wisdom.

In the old days Kuei Shan asked Lazy An, "What work do
you do during the twenty-four hours of the day?" An said, "I
tend an ox." Kuei Shan said, "How do you tend it?" An said,
"Whenever it gets into the grass, I pull it back by the nose."
Kuei Shan said, "You're really tending the ox!" People who
study the Path, in controlling wrong thoughts, should be like
Lazy An tending his ox; then gradually a wholesome ripening
will take place of itself.

4 **"Do not grasp another's bow"**

"Do not grasp another's bow, do not ride another's horse, do
not meddle in another's affairs." Though this is a commonplace saying, it can also be sustenance for entering the Path.
Just examine yourself constantly: from morning to night, what
do you do to help others and help yourself? If you notice even

the slightest partiality or insensitivity, you must admonish yourself. Don't be careless about this!

In the old days Ch'an Master Tao Lin lived up in a tall pine tree on Ch'in Wang Mountain; people of the time called him the "Bird's Nest Monk." When Minister Po Chu-yi was commander of Ch'ien T'ang, he made a special trip to the mountain to visit him. Po said, "It's very dangerous where you're sitting, Ch'an Master." The Master said, "My danger may be very great, Minister, but yours is even greater." Po said, "I am commander of Ch'ien T'ang: what danger is there?" The Master said, "Fuel and fire are joined, consciousness and identity do not stay: how can you not be in danger?"

Po also asked, "What is the overall meaning of the Buddhist Teaching?" The Master said, "Don't commit any evils, practice the many virtues."* Po said, "Even a three-year-old child could say this." The Master said, "Though a three-year-old child can say it, an eighty-year-old man cannot carry it out." Po then bowed and departed.

Now if you want to save mental power, do not be concerned with whether or not a three-year-old child can say it, or whether or not an eighty-year-old man can carry it out. Just don't do any evil and you have mastered these words. They apply whether you believe or not, so please think it over.

If worldly people whose present conduct is without illumination would correct themselves and do good, though the goodness is not yet perfect, isn't this better than depravity and shamelessness? One who does evil on the pretext of doing good is called in the Teachings one whose causal ground is not genuine, bringing on crooked results. If, with a straightforward mind and straightforward conduct, you are able to seize supreme enlightenment

---

* This is a very ancient saying in Buddhism, dating back to the Pali Canon. Usually a third part is added: ". . . and purify the mind; this is the teaching of all the buddhas."

4

directly, this can be called the act of a real man of power. The concerns that have come down from numberless ages are only in the present: if you can understand them right now, then the concerns of numberless ages will instantly disperse, like tiles being scattered or ice melting. If you don't understand right now, you'll pass through countless eons more, and it'll still be just as it is. The truth that is as it is has been continuous since antiquity without ever having varied so much as a hairsbreadth.

Matters of worldly anxieties are like the links of a chain, joining together continuously without a break. If you can do away with them, do away with them immediately! Because you have become habituated to them since beginningless time, to the point where they have become totally familiar, if you don't exert yourself to struggle with them, then as time goes on and on, with you unknowing and unawares, they will have entered deeply into you. Finally, on the last day of your life, you won't be able to do anything about it. If you want to be able to avoid going wrong when you face the end of your life, then from now on whenever you do anything, don't let yourself slip. If you go wrong in your present doings, it will be impossible not to go wrong when you're facing death.

There's a sort of person who reads scriptures, recites the Buddha-name, and repents in the morning, but then in the evening runs off at the mouth, slandering and vilifying other people. The next day he does homage to Buddha and repents as before. All through the years till the end of his life he takes this as daily ritual—this is extreme folly. Such people are far from realizing that the Sanskrit word *kshama** means to repent faults. This is called "cutting off the continuing mind." Once you have cut it off, never continue it again; once you have

---

* The Chinese has the Sanskrit word in transliteration: *kshama* means forgiveness; this repentance formally means confession of faults, or of transgression of the precepts in the case of monks and nuns, who met fortnightly in the ancient Buddhist communities in India for confession and repentance.

repented, do not commit (wrongdoings) again—this is the meaning of repentance according to our Buddha, which good people who study the Path should not fail to know.

The mind, discriminating intellect, and consciousness of students of the Path should be quiet and still twenty-four hours a day. When you have nothing to do, you should sit quietly and keep the mind from slackening and the body from wavering. If you practice to perfection over a long long time, naturally body and mind will come to rest at ease, and you will have some direction in the Path. The perfection of quiescence and stillness indeed settles the scattered and confused false consciousness of sentient beings, but if you cling to quiescent stillness and consider it the ultimate, then you're in the grip of perverted "silent illumination" Ch'an.

The Sanskrit word *prajna* means wisdom. Those who lack clear *prajna* and are greedy, wrathful, stupid, and lustful, those who don't have clear *prajna* and harm sentient beings, those who do such things as these—they are running away from *prajna*. How can this be called wisdom?

By keeping mindful of the matter of birth and death, your mental technique is already correct. Once the mental technique is correct, then you won't need to use effort to clear your mind as you respond to circumstances in your daily activities. When you don't actively try to clear out your mind, then you won't go wrong; since you don't go wrong, correct mindfulness stands out alone. When correct mindfulness stands out alone, inner truth adapts to phenomena; when inner truth adapts to events and things, events and things come to fuse in inner truth. When phenomena fuse with their inner truth, you save power; when you feel the saving, this is the empowerment of studying the Path. In gaining power you save unlimited power; in saving power you gain unlimited power.

This matter may be taken up by brilliant quick-witted folks, but if you depend on your brilliance and quick wits, you won't be able to bear up. It is easy for keen and bright people to enter, but hard for them to preserve it. That's because generally their entry is not very deep and the power is meager. With the intelligent and quick-witted, as soon as they hear a spiritual friend mention this matter, their eyes stir immediately and they are already trying to gain understanding through their mind's discriminating intellect. People like this are creating their own hindrances, and will never have a moment of awakening. "When devils from outside wreak calamity, it can still be remedied," but this (reliance on intellectual discrimination) amounts to "When one's own family creates disaster, it cannot be averted." This what Yung Chia meant when he said, "The loss of the wealth of the Dharma and the demise of virtue all stem from mind's discriminating intellect."*

---

* This refers to the Eighth, Seventh, and Sixth Consciousnesses—different names for a single thing, according to the *Consciousness Only Treatise*. Since Ta Hui regularly uses these three terms en bloc in this book, there's no need to enter deeply into the various schemes of contrasts and relationships among these three aspects that have been propounded in Buddhist theory. However, to give a rough indication: The first five consciousnesses (associated with the familiar five senses) become attached to sense objects because of the Sixth Consciousness, which discriminates among them. The Seventh Consciousness, the one that thinks and calculates, clings to the discriminations of the Sixth Consciousness, assumes the existence of a self, and plans actions good and evil, thus creating karma, bringing on birth and death, and obscuring the true nature of the Eighth Consciousness. The Eighth Consciousness is called Mind, the Seed Consciousness, and the Storehouse Consciousness: it is the all-encompassing basis, that which is influenced and transformed by the deluded Sixth and Seventh to form the substance of the experience of illusion. It's True Mind that does not keep to its own inherent nature, but transforms according to causal conditions pure or defiled, merged with them yet not merged: it's the "mind" and "consciousness" of the saying, "The triple world is only mind, the myriad things are only consciousness." With enlightenment, the eight consciousnesses are said to be transformed into four corresponding kinds of wisdom, or knowledge—for example, the Eighth Consciousness becomes the Great Perfect Mirror Wisdom. Yet even this transformation that comes with buddhahood is called "Changing names, not changing essence."

5   The Mind's Conceptual Discrimination

The obstruction of the Path by the mind and its conceptual discrimination is worse than poisonous snakes or fierce tigers. Why? Because poisonous snakes and fierce tigers can still be avoided, whereas intelligent people make the mind's conceptual discrimination their home, so that there's never a single instant, whether they're walking, standing, sitting, or lying down, that they're not having dealings with it. As time goes on, unknowing and unawares they become one piece with it—and not because they want to, either, but because since beginningless time they have followed this one little road until it's become set and familiar. Though they may see through it for a moment and wish to detach from it, they still can't. Thus it is said that poisonous snakes and fierce tigers can still be avoided, but the mind's conceptual discrimination truly has no place for you to escape.

6   There is Nothing to Attain

Gentlemen of affairs often take the mind (which assumes) there is something to attain to seek the Dharma (wherein) there is nothing to attain. What do I mean by "the mind (which assumes) there is something to attain"? It's the intellectually clever one, the one that ponders and judges. What do I mean by "the Dharma (wherein) there is nothing to attain"?

It's the imponderable, the incalculable, where there's no way to apply intelligence or cleverness.

Haven't you read of old Shakyamuni at the Assembly of the Lotus of the True Dharma? Three times Shariputra earnestly entreated him to preach, but there was simply no way for him to begin. Afterwards, using all his power, he managed to say that this Dharma is not something that can be understood by thought or discrimination. This was old Shakyamuni taking this matter of its ultimate conclusion, opening the gateway of expedient means* as a starting point for the teaching of the true nature of reality.

In the old days Hsueh Feng, the "Truly Awakened Ch'an Master," was so earnest about this matter that he went to Mt. T'ou Tzu three times and climbed Mt. Tung Shan nine times. Circumstances were not met for him (in those places, however) so later when he heard of the teaching of Chou, master of the Adamantine Wisdom Scripture, on Te Shan, he went to his abode. One day he asked Te Shan, "In the custom of the school that has come down from high antiquity, what doctrine is used to instruct people?" Te Shan said, "Our school has no verbal expression, nor does it have any doctrine to teach people." Later Hsueh Feng also asked, "Do I have any share in the business of the vehicle of this ancient school?" Te Shan picked up his staff and immediately hit him saying, "What are you saying?" Under this blow Hsueh Feng finally smashed the lacquer bucket (of his ignorance). From this we observe that in this sect intelligence and cleverness, thought and judgment, are of no use at all.

An ancient worthy had a saying: "Transcendent wisdom is

---

* Expedient means for expressing the ineffable and liberating sentient beings. Kuei Shan said, "The ultimate ground of reality does not admit a single atom, but in the gateways of myriad practices, not a single method (or thing) is abandoned."

like a great mass of fire. Approach it and it burns off your face." If you hesitate in thought and speculation, you immediately fall into conceptual discrimination. Yung Chia said, "Loss of the wealth of the Dharma and destruction of virtue all stems from the mind's conceptual discrimination." Hence we know that mind's conceptual discrimination not only obstructs the Path, but also can make people mistaken and confused, so they do all kinds of things that are no good.

Once you have the intent to investigate this Path to the end, you must settle your resolve and vow to the end of your days not to retreat or fall back so long as you have not yet reached the Great Rest, the Great Surcease, the Great Liberation. There's not much to the Buddha Dharma, but it's always been hard to find (capable) people. The concerns of worldly passions are like the links of a chain, joining together without a break. Those whose resolve is weak and inferior time and time again willingly become involved with them: unknowing and unawares they are dragged along by them. Only if the person truly possesses the faculty of wisdom and willpower will he consent to step back and reflect.

Yung Chia also said, "The real nature of ignorance is identical to the nature of enlightenment; the empty body of illusory transformations is identical to the Body of Reality. Once you've awakened, there's not a single thing in the Body of Reality. Original inherent nature is the naturally real enlightened one." If you think like this, suddenly, in the place where thought cannot reach, you will see the Body of Reality in which there is not a single thing—this is the place for you to get out of birth and death. What I said before, that one cannot seek the Dharma which has nothing to attain with the attitude that there is something to attain, is just this principle.

Gentlemen of affairs make their living within the confines of thought and judgment their whole lives: as soon as they hear a man of knowledge speak of the Dharma in which there is nothing to attain, in their hearts there is doubt and confusion, and they fear falling into emptiness. Whenever I see someone talking like this, I immediately ask him, is this one who fears falling into emptiness himself empty or not? Ten out of ten cannot explain. Since you have always taken thought and judgment as your nesting place, as soon as you hear it said that you shouldn't think, immediately you are at a loss and can't find your grip. You're far from realizing that this very lack of anywhere to get a grip is the time for you to let go of your body and your life.

Tun-li, my friend in the Path, when we met in Pien in 1126 you were of mature age and already knew of the existence of the Great Matter. But with your vast erudition you have entered too deeply into the Nine (Confucian) Classics and the Seventeen Histories; you are too brilliant and your lines of reasoning are too many, whereas your powers of stable concentration are too few. You are being dragged along by your daily activities as you respond to circumstances: thus you are unable to make a clean break right where you stand.

If correct mindfulness is present at all times, and the attitude of fear for birth and death doesn't waver, then, over long days and months, what was unfamiliar will naturally become familiar, and what was stale will naturally become fresh. But what is the stale? It's the brilliance and cleverness, that which thinks and judges. What is the unfamiliar? It's enlightenment, nirvana, true thusness, the buddha-nature—where there's no thought or discrimination, where figuring and calculating cannot reach, where there's no way for you to use your mental arrangements.

Suddenly the time arrives: you may be on a story of an ancient's entry into the Path, or it may be as you are reading the scriptures, or perhaps during your daily activities as you respond to circumstances; whether (your condition) is good or not good, or your body and mind are scattered and confused, whether favorable or adverse conditions are present, or whether you have temporarily quieted the mind's conceptual discrimination—when you suddenly topple the key link, there'll be no mistake about it.

To Li Hsien-ch'en

7 See the Moon, Forget the Pointing Finger

A gentleman reads widely in many books basically in order to augment his innate knowledge. Instead, you have taken to memorizing the words of the ancients, accumulating them in your breast, making this your task, depending on them for something to take hold of in conversation. You are far from knowing the intent of the sages in expounding the teachings. This is what is called counting the treasure of others all day long without having half a cent of your own. Likewise in reading the Buddhist Scriptures: you must see the moon and forget the fingers.* Don't develop an understanding based on the words. An ancient worthy said, "The buddhas expounded all teachings to save all minds; I have no mind at all, so what's the use of all the teachings?" If they can be like this when reading the scriptures, only then will people with resolve have some comprehension of the intent of the sages.

---

* In the Surangama Sutra it is said that the Buddhist Teachings are like a finger pointing at the moon (the truth, reality); once the moon is seen, the finger is of no further use. Ch'an masters often used this metaphor, and in fact the book from which these notes of Ta Hui are translated is entitled *Records of Pointing at the Moon.*

8   Stories and Sayings

These days in the Ch'an communities they use the extraordinary words and marvelous sayings of the ancients to question and answer, considering them situations for discrimination and beguiling students. They are far from getting to the root of their reality. When the buddhas preached the Truth, their sole concern was that people wouldn't understand; though they had recondite and obscure things to say, they would then bring in other comparisons and similes, to make sentient beings wake up and understand. For example, a monk asked Ma Tsu, "What is Buddha?" and Ma Tsu said, "Mind itself is Buddha." At this the monk was enlightened and entered (the Path): what discrimination is there here? But if the monk hadn't awakened from this, then this very "Mind itself is Buddha" would have been a situation of discrimination.*

When people engaged in meditation read the scriptural teachings and the stories of the circumstances in which the ancient worthies entered the Path, they should just empty their minds. Don't look for the original marvel or seek enlightenment in sounds, names, and verbal meanings. If you take this attitude, you're obstructing your own correct knowledge and perception, and you'll never have an entry. P'an Shan said, "It's like hurling a sword at the sky: no talk of whether it reaches or not!" Don't be careless! Vimalakirti said that the Truth goes beyond eyes, ears, nose, tongue, body, and intellect.

---

* In "meditation in which one contemplates sayings," *k'an hua ch'an,* the saying or story focused on (likely to be one of the famous "public cases" of Ch'an—a *kung an* or *koan*) is called *yin yuan,* "(a set of) causes and conditions," and hence "an incident," "a situation." If not used to their proper end, such meditation topics themselves can become objects of more discrimination.

If you want to penetrate this Truth, first you must clear out the gates of the six senses, leaving them without the slightest affliction. What does "affliction" mean? It means to be turned around by form, sound, scent, taste, touch, and phenomena, and not detaching from them. It's seeking knowledge and looking for understanding in the words and phrases of the scriptural teachings and the ancient worthies. If you can avoid giving rise to a second thought about the scriptural teachings or the stories of the ancient worthies entering the Path, and realize directly what they go back to, then there will be nothing in your own realm or in the realms of others that is not according to your will, nothing of which you are not the master.

Te Shan would see a monk enter the door and immediately strike him with his staff; Lin Chi would see a monk enter the door and immediately shout. Venerable adepts everywhere call this bringing it up face to face, imparting it directly, but I call it first class trailing mud and dripping water.* Even if you can take it up with your whole being at a single blow or shout, already you are not a man of power—(in fact) you have been doused over the head by someone else with a ladleful of foul water. How much the more so, if at a shout or blow you are looking for marvels or seeking subtle understanding—this is the stupidest of the stupid.

---

* Trailing mud and dripping means getting involved, going to lengths. It can refer to expression of compassion and resort to expedient liberating technique, or to confusion and delusion, "getting carried away."

9 Enlightenment and Delusion

In the old days the military commander Li Wen-ho studied with the Ch'an Master Ts'ung of Tz'u Chao at Shih Men and awakened to the essence of the Lin Chi School. He had a verse which said:

> To study the Path, one must be an iron man:
> Get hold of the mind and settle the issue immediately!
> Directly seizing supreme enlightenment,
> Don't concern yourself at all with right and wrong.

How marvelous these words are! They should be considered an aid for making the seeds of illumination unfold their potential.

"Buddha" is the medicine for sentient beings; once the disease of sentient beings is removed, the medicine has no further use. If the disease is removed but the medicine kept, though you enter the realm of enlightenment (buddhahood), you are unable to enter the realm of delusion (Mara).* This disease is equal to the disease of sentient beings before it is removed. When the disease is cured and the medicine removed, and both buddhahood and deluding influences are swept away entirely, only then will you have a bit of Accord with the causes and conditions of This Great Matter.

---

* *Mara* as a personal name refers to the lord of the heavens of desire, "The Killer." Taken from Sanskrit into Chinese, it took on the wider meaning of "demon," "devil," "nuisance," "hindrance." Anything that becomes the object of craving, anger, or confusion can be *mara*. Thus the Hua Yen Scripture includes among deluding influences good faculties, states of concentration, the spiritual friend and guide, and even the knowledge of the Truth that comes with enlightenment, when these become objects of clinging the learner is unwilling to part with.

Buddhas are those who have comprehended and completed things in the realm of sentient beings; sentient beings are those who have not comprehended and completed things in the realm of buddhas. If you want to attain Oneness,* just give up both buddhas and sentient beings at once: then there is no "comprehended and completed" or "not comprehended and completed."

An ancient worthy said, "Just perceive nothingness in the midst of things. When seeing form and hearing sound, don't be blind and deaf." This man knew the truth that the contrivances of the worldly are empty, false, and unreal. When he was faced with situations and circumstances as they suddenly popped up in front of him, he didn't go along with them, so they were taken under control by him.

In general, since time without beginning, you have overdone the familiar and left undone the unfamiliar. Even though you may see through it all for a moment, in the end your power in the Path cannot overcome the power of your acts (karma). And what is the power of acts? It is what's familiar and stale. And what is the power of the Path? It is what's unfamiliar and fresh. Basically however, there is no fixed measure to "the power of the Path" and "the power of acts." Just observe whether or not you are befuddled in the conduct of your daily activities. When you becloud the power of the Path, then it is overcome by the power of acts; when the power of acts prevails, then you get stuck wherever you go. When you get stuck wherever you go, then you become attached everywhere; when you get attached everywhere, you consider misery to be happiness. This is why Shakyamuni said to "The Kindly One" (foremost among his chief disciples in expounding the Dharma): "You use the characteristics matter and emptiness to overturn

---

* "Oneness," or "One Suchness." See below, page 86.

and eliminate each other in the Repository of Thusness,* and the Repository of Thusness accordingly becomes matter or emptiness, extending everywhere throughout the cosmos. For this reason, within it, the wind stirs and the air clears, the sun is bright and the clouds are dark."

Sentient beings, stifled by delusion, turn their backs on enlightenment and join the dusts, thus giving rise to sensory affliction and the existence of worldly forms. These are the ones who dim the power of the Path and are overcome by the power of their actions. Old Shakyamuni also said, "I formed the Repository of Thusness with subtle illumination, that is neither destroyed nor born; and the Repository of Thusness is only the illumination of sublime enlightenment shining throughout the whole cosmos." This is why within it the one is infinite and infinity is one, why the great appears within the small and the small appears within the great. The immutable field of enlightenment pervades all worlds in all directions and one's body contains a limitless space in all directions. On the tip of a hair you manifest the Land of the Jewel King and sitting within an atom of dust you turn the Great Wheel of the Dharma. This is not dimming the power of the Path in one's activities, and mastering the power of actions.

---

* According to Buddhist teaching, "both" the unconditioned, unchanging Mind of True Thusness "and" the myriad phenomena of cause and effect have one and the same essential inherent nature. To arouse sentient beings, provisionally it is said that the ordinary "reality" created and experienced by the mind of delusion—the familiar world of internal self, external objects—obscures and hides the true body of reality, which remains immanent, to be revealed by enlightenment. The term "Repository of Thusness" expresses the identity and fusion of both sides, that reality is neither worldly nor world-transcending, that deluded sentient beings are inherently enlightened and conditioned phenomena in flux are quiet and still as nirvana by nature. Three senses are combined in this term: "contained": Thusness is immanent in the world and enlightenment in beings—all things "contain" Thusness; "hidden": Thusness is obscured

Nevertheless, both are ultimately empty falsehoods. If one abandons the power of actions to grasp the power of the Path, then I would say that this person does not understand the skill in means of all the buddhas in expounding the truth as is appropriate to the occasion. Why? Have you not read how old Shakyamuni said, "If you cling to the truth aspect, you are attached to self, personality, living beings, and life;* if you cling to the non-truth aspect, you are attached to self, personality, living beings, and life." Therefore you should not cling to truth (Dharma), and you should not cling to what is untrue (adharma)—this is what I said before, that basically "the power of the Path" and "the power of actions" have no fixed measure. If you are a real man of wisdom, you will use the power of the Path as an instrument to clear away the power of habitual action. Once the power of actions has been cleared away, the Path too is empty and false. Thus it is said, "(The Buddha) only uses provisional terms in guiding sentient beings."

Before you've managed to see through it, you're beset with countless difficulties; after you see through it, what difficulty or ease is there? As Layman P'ang said,

The capacity of ordinary people's will is meager:
Falsely they say there is difficulty and ease.
Detached from form, empty as space,
You reach complete accord with the wisdom of the
    buddhas.

---

by affliction; "container": Thusness contains all the qualities of buddha-hood, and indeed "contains" everything.

* In the Complete Enlightenment Scripture, Buddha says, "Since time without beginning, all sentient beings have falsely imagined and clung to the existence of self, personality, living beings, and life, and accepted the four mistaken ideas as the substance of a real 'I.' Further, from this, hate and love are produced—within empty falsehood, clinging anew to empty falsehood. . . . Since there are false acts (karma), they falsely perceive the life cycle."

The form of discipline too is empty as space:
Deluded people consider themselves as upholding it.
Unwilling to pull out the root of the sickness,
They just fool with the flowery branches.

Do you want to know the root of the sickness? It's nothing else, just this clinging to difficulty and ease, arbitrarily giving rise to grasping and rejection. If this root of disease is not utterly extirpated, you will float and sink in the sea of birth and death without ever getting out.

As soon as the source of the sickness was pointed out to him by an old adept, Chang Ch'o, the famous scholar in the old days, understood enough to say:

Trying to eliminate passion aggravates the disease;
Rushing towards True Suchness is also wrong.
There is no obstruction in worldly circumstances according
to one's lot:
"Nirvana" and "birth and death" are equally illusions.

If you want to cut directly through, don't entertain doubts about buddhas and ancestral teachers, or doubts about birth and death—just always let go and make your heart empty and open. When things come up, then deal with them according to the occasion. Be like the stillness of water, like the clarity of a mirror, (so that) whether good or bad, beautiful or ugly approach, you don't make the slightest move to avoid them. (Then) you will truly know that the mindless world of spontaneity is inconceivable.

10   Lecture at the request of Wei Ch'iang

Do you want to know what truth is? It's True Thusness, Buddha-nature, Enlightenment, Nirvana. Do you want to know what the disease is? It's arbitrary conception, inverted thoughts and perceptions, greed, hatred, erroneous views. Even so, apart from the inversions of arbitrary conceptions there is no Truly So Buddha-nature; apart from greed, hatred, and erroneous views, there is no Enlightenment or Nirvana.

But say, is it right to separate them, or is it right not to separate them? If you separate them, keep one and get rid of the other, then the disease becomes even worse. If you do not separate them, this is truly presuming on the Buddha-nature and confusing True Thusness. In the end, how can one expound a principle whereby the disease is removed but the truth is not removed?

Some folks hear such talk and immediately say, "The truth itself is the disease—the disease itself is the truth—there is only verbal expression, no real meaning at all. Go along with True Thusness, and then inverted arbitrary conceptions, greed, hatred, and false views are all the truth. If you go along with error, then True Suchness, Buddha-nature, Enlightenment, and Nirvana are all disease." With such an understanding, don't say that you wear the patchwork robe—you are not even fit to be a lecturer's servant. Why? You should know that on the level ground the dead people are countless: obviously those who can pass through the forest of thorns are the adepts.*

Haven't you seen the saying of the man of old? "Even if there were something surpassing nirvana, I would say that it too is like a dream, an illusion." If in the midst of dreamlike

---

* The "level ground" is emptiness; "the forest of thorns" refers to delusion.

illusion, you are able to witness it as it really is, to understand it as it really is, to work on it as it really is, and to act on it as it really is, then you can use the method of according with reality to subdue yourself, and arousing an attitude of great compassion, create all kinds of skillful expedients whereby you can also subdue all sentient beings: and yet you entertain no notions of subduing or not subduing towards sentient beings; you entertain no notions of erroneous imagination, nor of greed, hatred, or false views; you entertain no thoughts of True Thusness, Buddha-nature, Enlightenment, or Nirvana; you entertain no thoughts of removing the disease without removing the truth, nor of keeping one and getting rid of the other, nor of separating or not separating them. Once you no longer have any such conceptions, then the One Path is clear, the even sameness of liberation.

To Tseng T'ien-yu

11   Illusion

Speaking of "empty illusion," it is illusion when created and illusion when experienced too; it's illusion when you're knowing and aware, and illusion when you're lost in delusion too. Past, present, and future are all illusions. Today, if we realize our wrong, we take an illusory medicine to cure an equally illusory disease. When the disease is cured, the medicine is removed, and we are the same person as before. If (you think that) there is someone else or some special doctrine, then this is the view of a misguided outsider.

In the instant of Maitreya's finger-snap, Sudhana was even able to forget the meditative states fostered in him by all his teachers: how much more so the beginningless habit energy of empty falsehood and evil deeds! If you consider the mistakes which you committed in the past as real, then the world right in front of you now is all real, and even official position, wealth and status, gratitude and love, are all real.

To Secretary Lou

12 Dealing with Situations

Since we parted, I don't know whether or not you can avoid being carried away by external objects in your daily activities as you respond to circumstances, whether or not you can put aside your heap of legal documents as you look through them, whether or not you can act freely when you meet with people, whether or not you engage in vain thinking when you're where it's peaceful and quiet, whether or not you are thoroughly investigating This Matter without any distracted thoughts.

Thus Old Yellow Face (Buddha) has said, "When the mind does not vainly grasp past things, does not long for things in the future, and does not dwell on anything in the present, then you realize fully that the three times are all empty and still." You shouldn't think about past events, whether good or bad; if you think about them, that obstructs the Path. You shouldn't consider future events; to consider them is crazy confusion. Present events are right in front of you: whether they're pleasant or unpleasant, don't fix your mind on them. If you do fix your mind on them, it will disturb your heart. Just take everything in its time, responding according to circumstances, and you will naturally accord with this principle.

Unpleasant situations are easy to handle; pleasant situations are hard to handle. For that which goes against one's will, it boils down to one word: patience. Settle down and reflect a moment and in a little while it's gone. It's pleasant situations that truly give you no way to escape: like pairing magnet and iron, unconsciously this and that come together in one place. Even inanimate objects are thus: how much the more so for those acting in ignorance, with their whole beings making a living within it! In this world, if you have no wisdom, you will be dragged unknowing and unawares by that ignorance into a net; once inside the net, won't it be difficult to look for a way out? This is why an early sage said, "Having entered the world, leave the world completely"—this is the same principle. In recent generations there's been a type who lose track of expedient means in their practice. They always consider acting in ignorance to be "entering the world," so then they think of a forced pushing away as the act of "leaving the world completely." Are they not to be pitied? The only exceptions are those who have pledged their commitment, who can see through situations immediately, act the master, and not be dragged in by others.

Hence Vimalakirti said, "For those with the conceit of superiority, falsely claiming attainment, the Buddha just says that detachment from lust, hatred, and ignorance is liberation. For those with no conceit of superiority, the Buddha says that the inherent nature of lust, hatred, and ignorance is identical to liberation." If you can avoid this fault, so that in the midst of situations favorable or adverse there is no aspect of origination or demise, only then can you get away from the name "conceit of superiority" (applied to one who thinks he has attained but hasn't). Only this way can you be considered to have entered the world and be called a man of power.

What I've been talking about thus far is all my personal life experience: even right now I practice just like this. I hope that you will take advantage of your physical strength and health and also enter this stable equilibrium.

To Tseng T'ien-yu

13 Stillness and Commotion

Having read your letter carefully, I have come to know that you are unremitting in your conduct, that you are not carried away by the press of official duties, that in the midst of swift flowing streams you vigorously examine yourself. Far from being lax, your aspiration to the Path grows ever more firm as time goes on. You have fulfilled my humble wishes solidly and profoundly.

Nevertheless, worldly passions are like a blazing fire: when will they ever end? Right in the midst of the hubbub, you mustn't forget the business of the bamboo chair and reed cushion (meditation). Usually (to meditate) you set your mind on a still concentration point, but you must be able to use it right in the midst of the hubbub. If you have no strength amidst commotion, after all it's as if you never made any effort in stillness.

I have heard that there was some complicated situation in the past, and now you are experiencing the sadness of the outcome; alone, you do not dare to hear your fate. If you arouse this thought, then it will obstruct the Path. An ancient worthy said, "If you can recognize the inherent nature while going along with the flow, there is neither joy nor sorrow."

Vimalakirti said, "It's like this: the high plateau does not produce lotus flowers; it is the mire of the low swamplands that produces these flowers." The Old Barbarian (Buddha) said, "True Thusness does not keep to its own nature, but according to circumstances brings about all phenomenal things." He also said, "Proceeding to effect according to circumstances, it extends everywhere while always here upon this Seat of Enlightenment." Would they deceive people? If you consider quietude right and commotion wrong, then this is seeking the real aspect by destroying the worldly aspect, seeking nirvana, the peace of extinction, apart from birth and death. When you like the quiet and hate the hubbub, this is just the time to apply effort. Suddenly when in the midst of hubbub, you topple the scene of quietude—that power surpasses the (meditation) seat and cushion by a million billion times.

To K'ung Hui

14   Don't Cling to Stillness

Once you have achieved peaceful stillness of body and mind, you must make earnest effort. Do not immediately settle down in peaceful stillness—in the Teachings this is called "The Deep Pit of Liberation," much to be feared. You must make yourself turn freely, like a gourd floating on the water, independent and free, not subject to restraints, entering purity and impurity without being obstructed or sinking down. Only then do you have a little familiarity with the school of the patchrobed monks. If you just manage to cradle the uncrying child in your arms, what's the use?

15 Don't Pray for Relief

Lin Chi said, "If you can put to rest the mind that frantically seeks from moment to moment, you will be no different from old Shakyamuni Buddha." He wasn't fooling people. Even bodhisattvas of the seventh stage seek Buddha-knowledge without their minds being satisfied:* therefore it is called "affliction." Really there's no way to manage: it's impossible to apply the slightest external measure.

Several years ago there was a certain Layman Hsu who was able to find an opening; he sent me a letter expressing his understanding that said, "Empty and open in my daily activities, there's not a single thing opposing me; finally I realize that all things in the three worlds are fundamentally nonexistent. Truly this is peace and happiness, joyful liveliness, having cast it all away." Accordingly, I instructed him with a verse:

> Don't be fond of purity:
> Purity makes people weary.
> Don't be fond of joyful liveliness:
> Joyful liveliness makes people crazy.

---

* The Hua Yen Scripture propounds ten stages of bodhisattvahood. Only with the seventh "Far-Going" stage is the discriminating knowledge that clings to existence and nonexistence cut off. But at the seventh stage there's still agent and object, wisdom apart from the truth, and hence accomplishment. "Though entering the gate of knowledge of contemplating emptiness, they scrupulously cultivate merit. Though detached from the three worlds, they adorn the three worlds."

With the eighth stage, outward seeking ceases, and accomplishment is abandoned, even as the Dharma is actualized in this "Immovable" stage. All the great deeds of benefiting self and others are likened to what happens when a person dreams of drowning, and generates a great burst of energy and acts with expedient means to save himself, and thus by his efforts wakes up. After he awakens, his doings cease.

As water conforms to the vessel,
It accordingly becomes square or round, short or long.
As for casting away or not casting away,
Please think it over more carefully.
The three worlds* and myriad things
Are no refuge—where is there any home?
If you are just thus,
This is a great contradiction.
This is to inform Layman Hsu
That his own kin are creating disaster—
Open wide the Eye of the thousand sages,
And do not keep praying for relief.

To Huang Po-ch'eng

16 Emptying Mind and Objects

In the daily activities of a student of the Path, to empty objects
is easy, but to empty mind is hard. If objects are empty but
mind is not empty, mind will be overcome by objects. Just
empty the mind, and objects will be empty of themselves. If
the mind is already emptied, but then you arouse a second

---

* "The three worlds" can mean simply past, present, and future, but
more often refers to the worlds of desire, of form, and of the formless.
The realm of desire is the world sentient beings bind themselves to with
lust and wrath—heavens, hell, and earth. The form realm comprises various meditative states, detached from lower desires, where physical body
and world still remain. People are bound to the form realm because they
cling to their views, accepting their perceptions as true, and because they
cling to spiritual discipline, seeing in it a cause for what is actually cause-
less, enlightenment. In the formless realm, there's only consciousness
absorbed in meditation, and no physical world.

thought, wishing to empty its objects, this means that this mind is not yet empty, and is again carried away by objects. If this sickness is not done away with, there is no way to get out of birth and death. Haven't you seen the verse which Layman P'ang presented to Ma Tsu?

> In the ten directions, the same congregation:
> Each and every one studies non-doing.
> This is the place where buddhas are chosen:
> Minds empty, they return successful.

Once this mind is empty, then what is there outside of mind that can be emptied? Think it over.

To Chen-ju

17 Non-Duality

If your mind does not run off searching or think falsely or get involved with objects, then this very burning house of passion is itself the place to escape the three worlds. Didn't Buddha say, "Not depending on or abiding in any situation, not having any discrimination, one clearly sees the vast establishment of Reality and realizes that all worlds and all things are equal and nondual." Thus a bodhisattva of the "Far-Going" Stage goes beyond all in the Two Vehicles* by virtue of the power of

---

* "The Two Vehicles" are those of the shravakas and of the pratyeka-buddhas. They realize emptiness as the antithesis of the world, the shravakas from hearing the teaching of enlightenment, the pratyekabuddhas from their own observation of cause and effect. Like ordinary sentient beings, those in the Two Vehicles are not liberated: both are held back by

the knowledge and wisdom which he practices: though he has attained the Treasury of the Buddha-realm, yet to teach he appears in the realms of delusion; though he has transcended the ways of delusion, yet he appears to practice the stuff of delusion. Though he appears to act the same as outsiders, he does not abandon the Buddhist Teachings; though he appears to go along with all that is worldly, he's perpetually practicing all world-transcending ways. These are the real expedient devices within the burning house of passion.

If people who study transcendent wisdom (*prajna*) abandon these expedients and go along with passions, they will certainly be controlled by the demons of delusion. And while yielding to sense-objects, to impose theories and say that affliction is itself enlightenment and ignorance is itself great wisdom, to act in terms of existence with every step while talking of emptiness with each breath, without admonishing oneself for being dragged along by the power of habitual action, to go on and teach others to deny cause and effect—the vicious poison of misguided delusion has entered the guts of people who act like this. They want to escape from passion, but it's like trying to put out a fire by pouring on oil. Aren't they to be pitied?

Only having penetrated all the way through can you say that affliction is itself enlightenment and ignorance is identical to great wisdom. Within the wondrous mind of the original vast quiescence—pure, clear, perfect illumination—there is not a single thing that can cause obstruction. It is like the

---

objects: the ordinary run by clinging to them, the Two Vehicles by rejecting them. Those in the Two Vehicles loathe and fear birth and death, not comprehending that there's nothing outside mind. In contrast to bodhisattvas, they shun the world to seek extinction and peace; grasping their own experience of emptiness, they cannot mix in the world of delusion to help other beings towards liberation.

emptiness of space: even the word "Buddha" is something alien, to say nothing of there still being passions or afflictions as the opposite.

To Hsu Tun-chi

18   The Great Affair

This affair is like the bright sun in the blue sky, shining clearly, changeless and motionless, without diminishing or increasing. It shines everywhere in the daily activities of everyone, appearing in everything. Though you try to grasp it, you cannot get it; though you try to abandon it, it always remains. It is vast and unobstructed, utterly empty. Like a gourd floating on water, it cannot be reined in or held down. Since ancient times, when good people of the Path have attained this, they've appeared and disappeared in the sea of birth and death, able to use it fully. There is no deficit or surplus: like cutting up sandalwood, each piece is it.*

Where do the passions of birth and death arise from? Where can it be located when gathering the causes to produce the effect? Since there is no place to locate it, Buddha is illusion and Dharma is illusion; the three worlds, twenty-five states of being, the sense-organs, sense-objects, and consciousnesses are utterly empty. When you get to this realm, there's no place to put even the word "Buddha"; if even the word "Buddha" has no applicability, where is there True Thusness, Buddha Nature, Enlightenment, or Nirvana? Thus the Great Being Fu

---

* When fragrant sandalwood is cut up, each piece is fragrant.

said, "Fearing that people will give rise to a view of annihilation, we provisionally establish empty names."

Students of the Path who do not understand this principle are always going to the stories of people of old entering the Path looking for mysteries and subtleties and marvels, seeking interpretations and understanding. They are unable to see the moon and forget the pointing finger, unable to cut directly through with one blow. This is what Yung Chia called understanding the empty fist* as though there were actually something in it, falsely making up wonders within the senses and their objects. Such people vainly imprison themselves within the passions of the five clumps, the sense-organs, objects, and consciousnesses of sensation, the twenty-five states of being†—the Tathagata said they are to be pitied. Haven't you seen Yen T'ou's saying? "Just have no desires and depend on nothing, then you'll be capable of goodness."

All this time there's just been a lump of flesh born of your parents. Unless you come up with a bit of energy, it is subject to the control of others. What else is there outside the lump of flesh? What can you hold to be wonderful, mysterious, or marvelous? What can you take to be Enlightenment or Nirvana? What can you take to be True Thusness or Buddha-nature? You wanted to investigate this affair to the end, but from the first you have not gotten to the root of its reality—

---

* Buddha's teachings are all skillful expedients suited to the circumstances and potentials of the listeners. This is likened to holding out a closed fist as if it contained some treat, to pacify a crying child.
† The five "clumps" are the *skandhas,* the "aggregations," or "heaps": matter, sensation, perception, synthesizing functions (volition), and consciousness. The twenty-five states of being span the three worlds: in the world of desire, the evil planes of existence (in hell, as ghosts, animals, or ungodly beings), the human world, and the heavens of desire; in the realm of form, the various meditation heavens; in the formless realm, the four states of boundless emptiness, boundless consciousness, nothingness, and neither no thought nor not no thought.

you just wanted to seek knowledge and understanding from the public cases of the ancients. Even if you had a thorough knowledge and understanding of the entire Buddhist Canon, on the last day of your life, when birth-and-death comes upon you, you won't be able to use it at all.

There's another sort: as soon as they hear a wise advisor speak of such an affair, they still use their conceptual minds to figure it out and say, "If it's like this, then won't I fall into emptiness?" Ten out of ten gentlemen of affairs entertain this kind of view. I have no choice but to tell them, "You haven't ever reached emptiness, so what are you afraid of? It's as if you're trying to leap out of the water before the boat has capsized." When I see that they don't understand, I don't spare the mouth-work, but try once more to create trailing vines* for them: (I say,) "This one who fears falling into emptiness—has he been emptied or not? If your eyes aren't empty, how can you see forms? If your ears aren't empty, how can you hear sounds? If your nose isn't empty, how can you smell scents? If your tongue isn't empty, how can you taste flavors? If your body isn't empty, how can you feel contact? If your intellect isn't empty, how can you distinguish the myriad phenomena?"

Didn't Buddha say that there is no eye, ear, nose, tongue, body, or mind; no form, sound, scent, flavor, touch, or phenomena; no sense-organs or sense-objects or consciousnesses of sensation; no twenty-five states of being? Even shravakas, pratyekabuddhas, bodhisattvas, and buddhas, as well as the doctrines preached by Buddha—Enlightenment, Nirvana, True Thusness, Buddha-nature—along with those who expound these doctrines and those who listen to these doctrines, those who make up these teachings and those who accept these

---

* "Trailing vines" often connotes "complications," "further additions"—verbal pointers or any modes of teaching which the teacher lets out for the student to get hold of.

teachings—none of these exist. When you reach such a realization, do you call it empty or not empty? Do you call it buddha? bodhisattva? shravaka? pratyekabuddha? Do you call it Enlightenment or Nirvana? Do you call it True Thusness or Buddhanature? Let those who say they are intelligent and quick-witted and not fooled by others try to determine what's what here. If you can settle it correctly, you should stay in a grass hut (by yourself), and live beyond the gate (of the monastery). If you cannot determine for sure, just don't open your big mouth to speak of things that are beyond you.

When men of power want to investigate This One Great Affair to the end, they all break down their facades and with bold spirit draw their spines up straight. Do not go along with the feelings of others. Take your own constant point of doubt and stick it on your forehead. Always be as if you owed someone millions, with nothing to repay with when pressed for payment, fearful of humiliation by others. Only thus will you have some direction in the task of finding urgency where there is no urgency, getting busy where there is no pressure, and finding importance where there is no importance. Work diligently day and night: while eating and drinking, when joyful or angry, in clean places or unclean places, in family gatherings, when entertaining guests, when dealing with official business in your post, when concluding a betrothal—all of these are first-class times to make efforts to arouse and alert yourself and awaken.

In the old days, the military governor Li Wen-ho was able to study Ch'an and attain great penetration and great enlightenment while in the thick of wealth and rank. When Yang Wen-kung successfully studied Ch'an, he was dwelling in the Imperial Han Lin Academy. When Chang Wu-chin studied Ch'an, he was the minister for transport in Kiangsi. These three elders are examples of this "not destroying the worldly aspect while speaking of the real aspect." When has it ever been necessary to leave wife and children, quit one's job, chew on vegetable roots, and cause pain to the body? Those of inferior aspiration shun clamor and seek quietude: thence they enter the ghost cave of "dead tree Ch'an" entertaining false ideas that only thus can they awaken to the Path. Haven't you seen Layman P'ang's words:

Just have no mind in myriad things:
Then what hindrance is there when myriad things
    surround you?
The iron ox doesn't fear the lion's roar:
It's like a wooden man seeing a picture of flowers and
    birds—
The wooden man's body itself has no feelings,
And the painted birds aren't startled when meeting the
    man.
Mind and objects are Thus—only this is:
Why worry that the Path of Enlightenment will not be
    fulfilled?

If you can manage not to forget the matter of birth and death while in the midst of the passions of the world, then even though you do not immediately smash the lacquer bucket (of ignorance), nevertheless you will have planted deep the seed-wisdom of transcendental knowledge (*prajna*). In another lifetime you will appear and save your mental power. You won't fall into evil dispositions: you'll overcome that sinking down into the defilement of passion.

Not seeking escape, some say this affair should not be treated casually, and make of it an object of veneration and faith. Views like this are countless.

As a gentleman of affairs, your study of the Path differs greatly from mine as a homeleaver. Leavers of home do not serve their parents, and abandon all their relatives for good. With one jug and one bowl, in daily activities according to circumstances, there are not so many enemies to obstruct the Path. With one mind and one intent (homeleavers) just investigate this affair thoroughly. But when a gentleman of affairs opens his eyes and is mindful of what he sees, there is nothing that is not an enemy spirit blocking the Path. If he has wisdom, he makes his meditational effort right there. As Vimalakirti said, "The companions of passion are the progenitors of the Tathagatas: I fear that people will destroy the worldly aspect to seek the real aspect." He also made a comparison: "It's like the high plateau not producing lotus flowers: it is the mud of the low-lying marshlands that produces these flowers."

If you can penetrate through right here, as those three elders Yang Wen-kung, Li Wen-ho, and Chan Wu-chin did, your power will surpass that of us leavers of home by twenty-fold. What's the reason? We leavers of home are on the outside breaking in; gentlemen of affairs are on the inside breaking out. The power of one on the outside breaking in is weak; the power of one on the inside breaking out is strong. "Strong" means that what is opposed is heavy, so in overturning it there is power. "Weak" means what is opposed is light, so in overturning it there is little power. Though there is strong and weak in terms of power, what is opposed is the same.

To Tseng Shu-ch'ih

19 Nothing to Be Given

There has never been anything to give to people, only folks who have been able to point out the road for people. An ancient worthy said, "Having some attainment is the jackal's yelp; having no attainment is the lion's roar."

Buddha was someone who had mastered adaptation: in the course of forty-nine years, in more than three hundred and sixty assemblies where he taught the Dharma, he guided people according to their individual faculties. Thus he preached with One Voice through all realms, while sentient beings each obtained benefits according to their kind. It's like "One gust of the east wind, and the myriad grasses all bend down": the Dharma preached by the Buddha is also like this.

If he had had the intent to create benefit in all realms, then this would have been preaching the Dharma egotistically. To want to cause myriad beings to gain deliverance according to their kind—isn't this after all impossible? Haven't you read how Shariputra, at the assembly where the Perfection of Wisdom was preached, asked Manjusri, "Don't all buddhas, the Tathagatas, awaken to the realm of truth?" Manjusri said, "No, Shariputra. Even the buddhas cannot be found: how could there be buddhas who awaken to the realm of truth? Even the realm of truth cannot be found: how could it be realized by the buddhas?" See how those two men spurred each other on this way: when did they ever set their minds on anything? All the buddhas and all the ancestral teachers since antiquity have had a style like this in helping people. It's just that later descendants have lost the essence of the school and set up their own individual sects, making up strange things and concocting marvels.

20   Profound Clarity

I am giving you the name Chan-jan, "Profound Clarity." An ancestral teacher said, "As long as there is mental discrimination and calculating judgment, all the perceptions of one's own mind are dreams. If mind and consciousness are quiescent and extinct, without a single thought stirring, this is called correct awareness." Once awareness is correct, then in your daily activities twenty-four hours a day, when seeing form, hearing sound, smelling scent, tasting flavor, feeling touch, or knowing phenomena, whether walking, standing, sitting, or lying down, whether speaking or silent, active or still, there's nothing that's not profound clarity. And since you don't engage in wrong thinking, all is pure whether there is thinking or not. Once you've attained purity, when active you reveal the function of profound clarity, and when inactive you return to the essence of profound clarity. Though essence and function are distinguished, the profound clarity is one: like when you cut up sandalwood, each and every piece is sandalwood.

These days there's a kind of phony whose own standpoint is not genuine: they just teach people to control their minds and sit quietly, to sit to the point where the breath ceases. I call this lot pitiable. I'm asking you to meditate in just this way, but though I instruct you like this, it's just that there's no other choice. If there really were something to work on in meditation this way, it would defile you. This mind has no real substance: how can you forcibly bring it under control? If you try to bring it under control, where do you put it? Since there's no place to put it, there's no times or seasons, no past or present, no ordinary people or sages, no gain or loss, no quiet or confusion; there's no name of profound clarity and no essence of profound clarity and no function of profound clarity, no one who speaks thus of profound clarity and no one to hear such talk of profound clarity.

To Ch'en Ming-chung

21   Beginners' Disease

"Buddha preached all doctrines to save all minds; I have no mind at all, so what's the use of any doctrines?" Basically there is nothing in any doctrine, and no mind in mind. The emptiness of mind and things both is their real character. But these days students of the Path often fear falling into emptiness. Those holding such views misapprehend expedient means and take the disease for the medicine: they are to be pitied deeply. Therefore Layman P'ang said, "Don't be averse to falling into emptiness—falling into emptiness isn't bad." He also said, "Just vow to empty all that exists; don't make real that which doesn't exist." If you can see through this one saying, then the ignorance (born of) boundless evil deeds will instantly melt away and disperse. Even the whole great canon preached by the Tathagata cannot explain this one sentence.

If a person has certain faith, and knows that there is such a method of great liberation, and if in that knowing he turns the key of transcendence, then Layman P'ang's saying and the whole great canon preached by the Buddha are no different, without before or after, ancient or modern, lack or excess. Such a person neither sees that any doctrines exist nor sees that any minds exist: the world in all directions is empty and vast. But don't entertain the view of vast emptiness: if you hold this view then there is someone expounding emptiness and someone who hears emptiness being expounded, then there are all doctrines to be heard and all minds to be experienced. Once there is something to be heard and experienced, then within there is the realizing mind and without there is a "Dharma" to be realized. Unless this disease is removed, the Teachings call it expounding the Dharma egotistically; it's also called slandering the Buddha, Dharma, and Community. It also says in the Teachings, "If you cling to the aspect of Dharma, then you are attached to self, person, living beings, and life. If you cling to the aspect of anti-Dharma, then you're attached to self, person, living beings, and life." This is the same principle as what I said previously about having a realizing mind within and an external truth realized.

Buddhist disciple Ch'en, you have realized that personal existence is false and that things are illusory. Amidst illusory falsehood you were able to contemplate the saying "A dog has no Buddha-nature"—suddenly, while washing your face, you found your nose, and sent me a letter expressing your understanding, trying your hand at explaining Ch'an. This was like a three-day-old tiger cub who already has the spirit to devour an ox. The message conveyed therein, though, was like a lucky monkey hitting the ground with a stick: where it hit, it went in a few inches, but where it missed, it had no grasp (of the issue) at all. Though in the main your basis is already correct you are not yet clear about the Great Dharma—this is a common disease of beginners entering the Path. If you can realize such a thing, push it to one side, and take the essential gate of all the buddhas and ancestral teachers and shut it at once: only if you find a life on the other side of the Primordial Buddha will you gain mastery of the Dharma.

Old Shakyamuni Buddha said, "If you only praise the Buddha-Vehicle, sentient beings are submerged in suffering. Once you truly realize such matters as this, you can extend and fulfill what you yourself have realized. Therefore you will not be bound by things and you won't seek to escape from things: then this way is all right and not this way is all right too; this way or not this way, it's all all right." Whatever you say or do, you're like a strong man flexing his arm—you don't rely on anyone else's strength. Once the arrow has left the bowstring, it has no power to return. It's not forced, since the Dharma is as it is. Only when you've understood like this can you begin to say that there's no good or bad, no buddha or sentient beings, and so on. But right now, without being clear about the Great Dharma, if you say such things, then I'm afraid you fall into what Yung Chia called "Realizing emptiness, denying cause and effect—wild and reckless, incurring calamity." You shouldn't be unaware of this! Just get the root, don't worry about the branches. Over a long long time it will sink in thoroughly: don't worry that you won't attain oneness. Work on it!

22 See the Tathagata Everywhere

Buddha also said, "Do not see the Tathagata in one teaching, one phenomenon, one body, one land, or one sentient being. You should see the Tathagata everywhere in all places." "Buddha" means "enlightened awareness," meaning to be totally aware always in all places. "Seeing (the Tathagata) everywhere" means to see the original source of one's self, the naturally real Buddha of inherent nature: there is not a single time or place or teaching or phenomenon or body or land or world of sentient beings that it does not extend through. Sentient beings miss this and revolve in the routines of the three worlds, experiencing all kinds of suffering. Buddhas realize this and transcend the ocean of all existence, experiencing supreme wonderful bliss. Nevertheless, neither suffering nor bliss has any real substance: but since delusion and enlightenment are different, suffering and bliss go separate ways. Thus Tu Shun said, "When the body of reality revolves in the five paths,* it is called 'sentient beings.' When sentient beings appear, the body of reality does not appear."

Good and evil all arise from one's own mind. But tell me, besides your activities, thoughts, and discrimination, what do you call your own mind? Where does your mind come from? If you can discern where your own mind comes from, then boundless karmic obstruction will be cleared away instantly, and all sorts of marvels will come of themselves without being sought.

Where do we come from at birth? Where do we go at death? If you know where we come from and where we go, then you can be called a student of Buddha. Who is it who knows of birth and death? And who is it who experiences birth and death? Again: who is it who doesn't know where we come from and where we go? Who is it who suddenly realizes where he comes from and where he goes to? And who is it who, contemplating these words, blinks his eyes unable to understand, his belly churning up and down, as if a mass of fire were placed in his heart? If you want to know, just apprehend him at the point where he can't understand. If you can recognize him then, you'll know that birth and death surely have nothing to do with him.

Whenever you're reading the scriptures or the stories of the ancient worthies entering the Path, when your mind doesn't

---

* Tu Shun was the first ancestral teacher of Hua Yen Buddhism in China. The Buddha's body of reality is the absolute reality, the formless and unchanging essence of everything. "Within the pure body of reality, there's not a form that doesn't appear," according to the Hua Yen. The five paths are in hell, as hungry ghosts, as animals, as humans, and as demonic spirits.

understand clearly and it seems bewildering and stifling and flavorless, as if you're gnawing on an iron spike, this is just the time to apply effort: above all you must not give up. This is the place where conceptual knowledge doesn't operate, where thought doesn't reach, where discrimination is cut off and the path of reason is annihilated. Where you can always explain reasons and apply discrimination, this all pertains to emotional consciousness. Time and again people take this thief as their son. Don't be unaware of this!

To Li Shih-piao

23 Before Seeking

You've indicated you want me to instruct you by letter in the direct essentials. This very thought of seeking instruction in the direct essentials has already stuck your head into a bowl of glue. Though I shouldn't add another layer of frost to the snow, nevertheless where there's a question it shouldn't go unanswered. I ask you to abandon at once all the joy you've ever felt in reading the words of the scriptures yourself or when being aroused and instructed by others. Be totally without knowledge and understanding, as before, like a three-year-old child—though the innate consciousness is there, it doesn't operate. Then contemplate what's there before the thought of seeking the direct essentials arises: observe and observe. As you feel you're losing your grip more and more and your heart is more and more uneasy, don't give up and slack off: this is the place to cut off the heads of the thousand sages. Students of the Path often retreat at this point. If your faith is thoroughgoing, just keep contemplating what's before the thought of seeking instruction in the direct essentials arises. Suddenly you will awaken from your dream, and there won't be any mistake about it.

To Lu Shun-yuan

24 Don't Consciously Await Enlightenment

Whether you're happy or angry, in quiet or noisy places, you still must bring up Chao Chou's saying "A dog has no Buddha-nature." Above all, don't consciously await enlightenment. If you consciously await enlightenment, you're saying, "Right now, I'm deluded." If you wait for enlightenment clinging to delusion, though you pass through countless eons, you will still not be able to gain enlightenment. As you bring up the saying, just arouse your spirit and see what principle it is.

Constantly take the two concerns—not knowing where we come from at birth and not knowing where we go at death—and stick them on the point of your nose. Whether eating or drinking, whether in quiet or noisy places, you should make scrupulous efforts from moment to moment, always as if you owed someone millions with no way out, your heart sorely troubled, with no opening to escape. Searching for birth, it cannot be found; searching for death, it cannot be found—at such a moment, the roads of good and evil are immediately cut off. When your awareness has gotten like this, this is precisely the time to apply effort: contemplate the story right here.

A monk asked Chao Chou, "Does a dog have Buddha-nature or not?" Chao Chou said, "No." As you contemplate this, don't try to figure it out, don't try to explain it, don't demand clear understanding, don't take it verbally, don't construe the raising of it as the principle, don't fall into empty quiescence, don't consciously anticipate enlightenment, don't take your understanding from the explanations of the teachers of our school, don't drop it into the bag of unconcern. Whether walking, standing, sitting, or lying down, just constantly call the story to mind: "Does a dog have Buddha-nature or not? No." When you can keep your attention on it fully, when verbal discussion and intellectual consideration cannot reach and your heart is agitated, when it's like gnawing on an iron spike, without any flavor, then you must not falter in your intent—when you get like this, after all it's good news. Haven't you read the ancient worthy's saying?—"Buddha preached all teachings to save all minds; I have no mind at all, so what's the use of any teaching?" It's not just in the tradition of the Patriarchs that it's like this—the whole great canonical teaching spoken by the Buddha is also this same principle.

Sentient beings' obstruction by evil deeds is serious: no sooner do they get out of bed each day than their minds fly around in confusion. Thinking of fame and profit, they take up the false concepts of "others" and "self," continuing unbroken like the links of a chain from morning till night, without ever growing tired of it. If perchance they think of entering our school, they think about it intellectually and immediately want to understand it themselves. Since the judgments of the mind's conceptual discrimination do not apply here, they get annoyed and already want to give up, saying "What reason is there?" People like this are beyond counting.

But you are not this way, Shun-yuan, companion in the Path: knowing all the empty falsehoods of this defective world, with singleness of mind and intent, you want to understand where we come from when we're born and where we go to when we die right where you are. Since you don't know where we come from, you don't know where we go either. The clear solitary light, present right here, the one that distinguishes right and wrong, good and bad for people, decides what is and what is not, what's true and what's false. Wait till you're like a man drinking water who knows for himself whether it's cold or warm and doesn't accept the judgment in the mouth of someone else. Suddenly you will burst forth and reach the ultimate peace and bliss, the place of great rest and great surcease—then for the first time you give your own approval. It is for this that you have sought my instruction; I have taken up my pen and written freely, producing a bunch of trailing vines. However, things do not arise by themselves—there must be a reason. If you understand this only as creeping vines, entangling complications, how will you get it?

Haven't you read how in the old days Master Tzu Hu said, "The Ancestral Teacher's coming from the West only means that winter is cold and summer is hot, night is dark and day is light." It's just that you vainly set up meaning where there is no meaning, create concern where there is no concern, impose "inside" and "outside" where there is no inside or outside, and talk endlessly of this and that where nothing exists. Therefore your cessation cannot be perfectly clear, so that you cannot be independent of the senses and their objects. By this assessment, you have never come to my place seeking words of instruction, and I have never written a single word (for you). Winter's cold, summer's heat, night's darkness, day's light, inside, outside, in between, east, west, south, north have never varied, never increased or decreased the least little bit. What's the reason? "Our school has no words and phrases, nor is there any doctrine to give to people." Since there's not a single doctrine to give to people, what's this that's written here? And what is it that speaks of winter cold, summer heat, inside, outside, and in between? What is it that has never shifted east, west, south, or north a hairsbreadth? Bah!

Existence cannot be grasped; nonexistence cannot be grasped either. Winter's cold and summer's heat cannot be grasped; inside, outside, and in between cannot be grasped. The one who speaks like this cannot be grasped; the one who hears such talk cannot be grasped either. Not even a fine hair can be grasped. Neither you nor I can be grasped. Ungraspability itself also cannot be grasped. Amidst ungraspability, apprehending things this way, when you get to this point, how will you seek? Even this "how will you seek" has no applicability. Hence these words too are not acceptable. Since these words are not accepted, I certainly have nothing to say and you certainly have nothing to hear. "No speech is true speech and no hearing is true hearing." Thus I am you and you are me: we are not two, you and I. Because there's no duality, no distinction, and no separation, when the Colossus of Chia Chou eats yellow lotus, the Iron Ox of Shensi tastes the bitterness. Bitter, not bitter—clearly behold what cannot be seen. Bah!

To Ch'en Li-jen

25 Contemplating "No"

A monk asked Chao Chou, "Does a dog have Buddha-nature or not?" Chao Chou said, "No." This one word "no" is a knife to sunder the doubting mind of birth and death. The handle of this knife is in one's own hand alone: you can't have anyone else wield it for you: to succeed you must take hold of it yourself. You consent to take hold of it yourself only if you can abandon your life. If you cannot abandon your life, just keep to where your doubt remains unbroken for a while: suddenly you'll consent to abandon your life, and then you'll be done.

Only then will you believe that when quiet it's the same as when noisy, when noisy it's the same as when quiet, when speaking it's the same as when silent, and when silent it's the same as when speaking. You won't have to ask anyone else, and naturally you won't accept the confusing talk of false teachers.

During your daily activities twenty-four hours a day, you shouldn't hold to birth and death and the Buddha Path as existent, nor should you deny them as nonexistent. Just contemplate this: A monk asked Chao Chou, "Does a dog have Buddha-nature or not?" Chao Chou said, "No."

To Chang Yang-shu

26 Power

Old layman, your actions and behavior are in subtle accord with the Path, but you have not been able to get the burst of power. If in your daily activities responding to circumstances you do not stray from your past footsteps, though you haven't gotten the burst of power, still, on the last day of your life, the King of Death will have to fold his hands and submit. How much the more so if you reach the moment of realization!

Though I haven't seen you in person, as I consider the things you do, (I find that) you strike a balance between great and small, without any excess or insufficiency—this is where you accord with the Path. At this point, don't have any thoughts of affliction, and don't have any thoughts of the Buddha Dharma either: both the Buddha Dharma and afflictions are extraneous matters. Yet don't think of them as extraneous matters either. Just turn your light around and reflect back:

where does the one who entertains such thoughts come from? What shape does he have when acting? Once your tasks are taken care of according to your intentions, all thoroughly done without any lack or excess, at just such a time, whose power are you receiving? Meditate like this, and over the long days and months, it will be like a man learning archery: naturally he comes to hit the target.

"Sentient beings get inverted: they lose themselves and pursue objects." Addicted to their taste for petty desires, they willingly receive immeasurable suffering. Day after day, even before they've opened their eyes and gotten out of bed, while they're half awake and half asleep, their minds are already flying around in confusion, pursuing a torrent of vain thoughts. Although their good and bad doings are not yet manifest, before they've gotten out of bed heaven and hell have already instantly formed within their hearts. And when their actions do come forth, they've already fallen into the storehouse mind. Didn't Buddha say that all the senses are manifestations of one's own mind, that the physical body and organs are the appearances of one's own false thoughts? He established ways to show this, likening them to river currents, seeds, lamplight, wind, and clouds, changing and decaying from moment to moment, unsettled as monkeys, reveling in filth like flies, insatiable as flames fanned by the wind, turning like a waterwheel from the habit energy of beginningless falsity, and so on. If you can understand thoroughly like this, then it's called the knowledge that there's neither self nor others. Heaven and hell are nowhere else but in the heart of the person while he's half awake and half asleep, before he's gotten out of bed—they don't come from outside. When you're getting started but are not yet under way, when you're awakening but are not yet awake, you must diligently reflect back on this, but without struggling with it as you reflect back—if you struggle, you waste power. Didn't the Third Ancestral Teacher say so?—

"When you try to stop motion to return to stillness, the stopping causes further commotion."

As soon as you become aware of gradually conserving power in the midst of the afflictions of daily activities, this is where a person acquires power. This is how a person achieves buddhahood and becomes an ancestral teacher, this is how a person changes hell into heaven, this is where a person sits in peace, this is where a person gets out of birth and death, this is where a person becomes sovereign above the ancient emperors Yao and Shun, this is where a person raises the weary people from misery, this is where a person brings prosperity to his adopted descendants. At this point it's extraneous to speak of buddhas or ancestral teachers, of mind or nature, of the original or the wondrous, of principle or phenomena, or of good or bad. Since even these things are extraneous, how much more alien to agree to do things in passion which the former sages censured! If you don't even consent to do good, how can you consent to do what is not good? If you can believe in these words, this is what Yung Chia meant when he said, "Walking is also meditation; sitting is also meditation; speaking or silent, moving or still, the body is at rest." These are not empty words: please act according to them, without ever changing. Then, although you have not yet witnessed the scenery of your own fundamental state fully, though you have not yet seen your own original face clearly, what was raw will become ripe, and what was stale will become fresh. Be sure to remember: where you save power is where you gain power.

Every time I say this to people, it always seems that I've said it over and over. Most take it lightly, and won't consent to make it their task. You should try to work like this for only ten days or so, and then you will see for yourself whether you are saving power or not saving power, whether you are gaining power or not gaining power. You will be like someone who drinks water and knows for himself whether it is cold or warm—you cannot tell another person about it, you cannot show it to anyone. An ancient worthy said, "When you speak of realization, you cannot show it to others; when you speak of the truth, you cannot do it without realization." Only if you have realized and attained and believed and awakened to that which one must realize and attain and believe and awaken to for himself, do you reach tacit accord. If one has not realized and attained and believed and awakened, not only will he have no faith for himself, but also he'll not believe that anyone else has attained this realm.

Old Layman, by nature you are near to the Path: your present determined actions and conduct do not need any change. In comparison with other people, you've already gotten 9,999 parts out of ten thousand; you just lack that final burst of power.

Gentlemen of affairs who study the Path often understand rationally without getting to the reality. Without discussion and thought they are at a loss, with no place to put their hands and feet—they won't believe that where there is no place to put one's hands and feet is really a good situation. They just want to get there in their minds by thinking and in their mouths to understand by talking—they scarcely realize they've already gone wrong.

Buddha said, "The Tathagata uses all sorts of similes to explain all kinds of things, but there is no simile that can explain this Dharma. Why? Because the road of intellectual knowledge is cut off: (the Dharma) is inconceivable." Truly we know that thought and discrimination obstruct the Path. If you can cut off before and after, then the road of intellectual knowledge will be cut off by itself. If you can cut off the road of intellectual knowledge, then talk of all kinds of things is all this Dharma. Once this Dharma is clear, then this very clarity is the state of inconceivable great liberation. This state itself is impossible to conceive; since the state of inconceivable, all similes are also inconceivable, and all kinds of things are also inconceivable. And this inconceivability itself is also inconceivable. These words too are inapplicable, and this inapplicability is also inconceivable. Pushing on like this ever more exhaustively, whether it's things or the Dharma, similes or states, they are like a circle, with no starting point, no beginning and no end—all are the inconceivable Dharma.

Thus it is said that the abode of bodhisattvas is inconceivable, but therein thought is inexhaustible. When you've entered this inconceivability, thought and no-thought are both quiescent and extinct. Yet you should not abide in quiescent extinction, for if you do, you are being absorbed by the experience of the Dharma realm.* In the Teachings this is called affliction by the dust of the Dharma. Only when you have annihilated the experiences of the Dharma realm and all sorts of wonders are cleared away at once, should you look at such sayings as "What is the meaning of the coming from the West?—The cypress tree in the garden." "What is Buddha?—Three pounds of hemp.—A dry piece of shit." "A dog has no Buddha-nature." "Who does not keep company with the myriad things?—Swallow all the water in West River in one gulp, and I'll tell you." "Where do all the buddhas appear?—East Mountain walks on the water." When suddenly you can penetrate at a single phrase, only then is it called turning to the Dharma realm without experience. When you see it as it really is, practice according to reality and act according to

---

* In perfect enlightenment, quiescent extinction and universal awareness are not two. In realizing it there's no gain or loss, no grasping or abandoning; the one who realizes it is neither acting nor stopping. Since there's neither subject nor object in this realization, ultimately, there's no realization and no realizer—both birth and death and nirvana are like yesterday's dreams. But clinging to the Dharma is hard to wipe out: those who cannot eliminate it are called people who have fallen at the peak—they are afflicted by the dust of the Dharma. So even perfect realization of nirvana is still an egotistical view.

reality, then you can manifest the Jewel King's realm on the tip of a hair and turn the Wheel of the Great Dharma while sitting within an atom of dust. Then creating all things or destroying all things is entirely up to oneself. Like a strong man flexing his arm, you don't depend on the strength of others; like a lion strolling along, you won't seek companions. When all sorts of states of surpassing wonder appear before you, you won't marvel at them; when all sorts of states of evil deeds appear before you, you won't fear them. In the conduct of your daily activities, you will be abandoned and expansive, free and independent wherever you go.

Only if you arrive at this stage can you say there is no heaven or hell, and such things. Yung Chia said, "There are neither humans nor buddhas: the universe is like a bubble in the ocean, all the sages are like flashes of lightning." If he hadn't gotten to this stage, how could Yung Chia have said this? But with these words, those who misunderstand are many. Without penetrating to the source, you'll only produce verbal understanding and say that everything is nonexistent, denying cause and effect, considering the teaching expounded by all the buddhas and ancestral teachers as false and empty, saying they deceive and confuse people. If this disease is not removed, then you're "confused and reckless, inviting calamity." Buddha said, "False and fickle minds multiply their various clever views. If they don't apply existence, then they apply nonexistence. If they don't apply these two, then they try to figure it out somewhere between existence and nonexistence. Even if they see through this disease, they're sure to go wrong on 'neither existence nor nonexistence.' "

Thus the former sages took pains to admonish us, to have us detach from the four phrases and cut off their hundred negations, to make a clean break directly, think no more of before and after, and cut off the heads of the thousand sages. The four phrases are "it exists," "it doesn't exist," "it neither exists nor doesn't exist," and "if both exists and doesn't exist." Having penetrated these four phrases, when I see someone saying that all things really exist, I go along with it and talk existence, but without being obstructed by this "it really exists"; when I see someone saying that all things are really nonexistent, I go along with it and talk nonexistence, but not the nonexistence of the world is totally empty; when I see someone say that all things both exist and don't exist, I go along with it and talk both existence and nonexistence, but this is no sophistry; when I see someone say that all things neither exist nor don't exist, I go along with it and talk neither existence nor nonexistence, but this is no contradiction. It's this that Vimalakirti said: "Where the six outsiders fall, you fall along with them."

To Wang Yen-chang

27 Feelings and Affliction

I take it your fifth son is not recovering from his illness. You had thought that in this realm the feeling between a father and his son, the flow of affection over a thousand lives and a hundred ages, would be impossible. In the world of the five corruptions* all is empty and false: there's not one that's genuinely real. I ask you to contemplate this constantly, whether you're walking, standing, sitting, or lying down. Then gradually over time (your feelings) will be worn away. Nevertheless, it is precisely when afflicted that you should carefully investi-

---

* The corruption of the age, the corruptions of the prevalent false views and afflictions, and the consequent corruption of sentient beings and the shortening of the life span.

gate and inquire where the affliction arises from. If you cannot get to the bottom of its origination, then where does the one who is afflicted right now come from? Right when you're afflicted, is it existent or nonexistent, empty or real? Keep investigating until your mind has nowhere to go. If you want to think, then think; if you want to cry, then cry. Just keep on crying and thinking. When you can arouse yourself to the point where the habit energy of love and affection within the Storehouse Consciousness is exhausted, then naturally it's like water being returned to water, giving you back your original being, without affliction, without thoughts, without sorrow or joy.

"Having entered the world, leave the world completely. Then worldly things are the Buddha Dharma and the Buddha Dharma is worldly things." Father and son are one by nature: is there such a thing as a father who is not troubled when his son dies and who doesn't think about him, or a son who isn't troubled when his father dies and doesn't think about him? If you try to suppress (such sentiments) forcibly, not daring to cry or think about it, then this is deliberately going against the natural pattern, denying your inherent nature; (it's like) raising a sound to stop an echo, or pouring on oil to put out a fire.

Right when you're afflicted, it's not at all something alien, and you shouldn't think of it as alien. Yung Chia said, "The real nature of ignorance is enlightenment; the empty body of illusory transformation is the Body of Reality." These words are genuine and true, not lies or falsehoods. If you can see completely like this, you couldn't think or be afflicted even if you wanted to. Contemplating like this is called correct contemplation; any other contemplation is called incorrect. Actually, it's before correct and incorrect are separated that you should apply effort. This is the truth as I have determined it—don't talk of it in front of people who have no wisdom.

28 Ignorance

In the conduct of their daily activities sentient beings have no illumination. If you go along with their ignorance, they're happy; if you oppose their ignorance, they become vexed. Buddhas and bodhisattvas are not this way: they make use of ignorance, considering this the business of buddhas. Since sentient beings make ignorance their home, to go against it amounts to breaking up their home; going with it is adapting to where they're at to influence and guide them.

29 Smashing Doubt

Right where you stand, investigate the one in you who covets wealth and rank: where does he come from, and, in the future, where will he go? Since you don't know where he comes from or where he goes, your mind will feel confused and unhappy. Right when you're confused and unhappy, it's not someone else's affair—right here is where to contemplate a saying.

A monk asked Yun Men, "What is Buddha?" Yun Men said, "A dry piece of shit." Just bring up this saying. When all your machinations suddenly come to an end, then you'll awaken. Don't seek to draw realization from the words or try in your confusion to assess and explain. Even if you could explain clearly and speak to the point, this would all be phantom plans. If your feelings of doubt are not smashed, birth and death goes on. If your feelings of doubt are smashed, then the mind of birth and death is cut off. When the mind of birth and death is cut off, views of Buddha and Dharma perish. With views even of Buddha and Dharma gone, how could you go on to create any views of sentient beings and affliction? Just take your confused unhappy mind and shift it into "A dry piece of shit." Once you hold it there, then the mind that fears birth and death, the mind that's confused and unhappy, the mind which thinks and discriminates, the mind that acts intelligent, will naturally no longer operate. When you become aware that it's not operating, don't be afraid of falling into emptiness. Suddenly, in holding firm (the mind to the saying), the scene is cut off, for an entire lifetime of unexcelled joy and happiness. When you've gotten the scene cut off, then when you arouse views of Buddha, Dharma, or sentient beings, when you think, discriminate, act intelligent, and explain principles, none of it interferes. In the conduct of your daily activities, just always let go and make yourself vast and expansive. Whether you're in quiet or noisy places, constantly arouse yourself with the saying "A dry piece of shit." As the days and months come and go, of itself your potential will be purified and ripen. Above all you must not arouse any external doubts besides: when your doubts about "A dry piece of shit" are smashed, then at once doubts numerous as the sands of the Ganges are all smashed.

30 Present Awareness and Comparative Awareness

Yen T'ou said, "In the future, if you want to propagate the Great Teaching, it must flow out point by point from within your own breast to cover heaven and earth: only then will it be the action of a man of power." Not only did these words of Yen T'ou's bring to light Hsueh Feng's basic capacity, but also they should serve for ten thousand generations as a standard for those who study the Path. That which flows out from one's own breast, as he calls it, is one's own beginningless present awareness,* fundamentally complete of itself. As soon as you arouse a second thought, you fall into comparative awareness. Comparative awareness is something gained from external refinements; present awareness is something from before your parents were born, something from the other side of the Primordial Buddha. Power gained within present awareness is strong; power gained from comparative awareness is weak. With strong power one can enter both enlightenment and delusion. If one's power is weak, he can enter the realm of enlightenment, but in the realm of delusion he always beats the drum of retreat—such people are countless.

This affair is not a matter of intelligence or acuity, nor does it lie in dull faculties and shallow understanding. Actually, it's just an abrupt bursting out that's the criterion. As soon as

---

* "Present awareness" means the immediate direct apprehension of the real nature of things, without affixing names and categories, without assessment, without giving rise to discrimination, without holding to them as external, according to the *Consciousness Only Treatise*. The actions of the buddhas are entirely present awareness. Yen Shou explains: "Turning against present awareness, you lose the essence of your own mind; pursuing comparative and wrong awareness, you falsely recognize external sense-objects. All day long you use mind to grasp mind, use illusion to take illusion as an object."

you've attained this scene, then whatever words and phrases you have, they're not established apart from the real. When where they're established is real, this is the so-called "flowing out from within one's own breast to cover heaven and earth." It's just like this; it's not making up sayings looking for something extraordinary, so other people will be speechless, and consider your beautiful thoughts and flowery speech and pointed new ideas as "flowing out from your breast."

To Ch'en Tzu-chung

31 Understand Right Where You Are

If you want to study this Path, you must understand right where you are. As soon as you rely on the slightest knowledge, you miss the scene right where you're standing. When you've completely comprehended the scene right where you are, then all kinds of knowledge—all without exception—are things right where you are. Thus the Ancestral Teacher said, "At the very moment one speaks of knowledge, knowledge itself is mind, and this very mind itself is knowledge." Since knowledge is right now, if right now you don't go another moment, but do away with your knowledge right where you are, then you'll join hands and walk along together with the ancestral teachers. If you cannot yet be like this, don't go wrong in your knowledge.

32 Thought after Enlightenment

When studying worldy things, one relies totally on verbal meanings and mental thoughts. But if you use verbal meanings and thoughts to study the world-transcending Dharma, you are way off. Didn't Buddha say so?—"This Dharma is not something that thought and discrimination can understand." And Yung Chia said, "The loss of the wealth of the Dharma and the demise of virtue all stems from mind's discriminating consciousness." This is because the mind's discriminating consciousness is the home of thought and discrimination.

If you're determined to take up this great affair, I ask you to boldly apply your spirit, and make a clean break with this, the root of birth and death and delusion, which comes as the vanguard and leaves as the rearguard: this is the time to appear. At just such a time, you can finally use verbal meanings and mental thoughts to effect. Why? Because once the Storehouse Consciousness has been cleared away, then birth and death and delusion have no place to stay. When birth and death and delusion have no home, then thinking and discrimination themselves are nothing but transcendent wisdom (*prajna*) and subtle knowledge: there's not the slightest thing further to obstruct you. Thus it is said:

> Observing the sequence of phenomena,
> Using wisdom to discriminate,
> Judging right and wrong—
> This doesn't go against the Seal of Truth.

When you've reached this stage, then even if you act smart and expound principles, it's all the great perfect peace of nirvana, the great ultimate, the realm of great liberation—there isn't anything else. So P'an Shan's saying, "A complete mind is buddha; a complete buddha is human"—means this.

If you're not yet like this, don't let your mind's discriminating consciousness have its way when you're walking, standing, sitting, and lying down. Over a long long time it will become completely purified; naturally, you shouldn't apply to push it away.

To Tseng T'ien-yu

33 Discriminating Consciousness and Wisdom

Constantly calculating and making plans, flowing along with birth and death, becoming afraid and agitated—all these are sentiments of discriminating consciousness. Yet people studying the Path these days do not recognize this disease, and just appear and disappear in its midst. In the Teachings it's called acting according to discriminating consciousness, not according to wisdom. Thereby they obscure the scenery of the fundamental ground, their original face.

But if you can abandon it all at once, so you neither think nor calculate, suddenly losing your footing as you tread upon your nostrils, then these very sentiments of discriminating consciousness are the subtle wisdom of true emptiness—there is no other wisdom that can be attained. If there were something attained and something realized besides, then it wouldn't be right. It's like a person when he's deluded calling east west, and when he's arrived at enlightenment, west *is* east—there is no other east. This subtle wisdom of true emptiness is coeval with the great void: is there a single thing within this great void that could obstruct it? The void is not subject to being obstructed by things, nor does it hinder the coming and going of all things within it. The subtle wisdom of true emptiness is also thus: birth and death, ordinary and holy, stains and defilements, cannot touch it at all. Although they can't touch it, the subtle wisdom does not hinder birth and death, ordinary and holy, from coming and going in its midst.

To Hsieh K'uo-jan

34   Be Unborn

The mind-fire is blazing: burning bright without a stop. Desire, hatred, and delusion continue it, joining together without a break like links of a chain. If you don't have a strong will, as the days and months go by, unawares you will be controlled by the delusive demons of form, sensation, perception, volition, and consciousness. If for a single moment you can be unborn amidst causal origination, then without leaving desire, hatred, and delusion, you use the seal of the demon kings to drive out all demons. Then you are considered a good spirit protecting the Dharma. And this won't be a forced action, since the Dharma is like this.

35 So Very Close

Just because it's so very close, you cannot get this Truth out of your own eyes. When you open your eyes it strikes you, and when you close your eyes it's not lacking either. When you open your mouth you speak of it, and when you shut your mouth it appears by itself. But if you try to receive it by stirring your mind, you've already missed it by eighteen thousand miles.

36 Neither Arousing nor Stopping False Thoughts

An ancient worthy had a saying: "Just accept (the Dharma) willingly: you certainly won't be deceived." You yourself probably cannot believe this fully. If you are taken over by external objects in your daily activities as you respond to circumstances, you won't be able to meditate with consistency: thus interruptions occur and during these breaks you won't avoid confusion and agitation in your heart. Yet this is a good time. It was this principle when Buddha said, "I dwell in all times without arousing false thoughts, and without putting a stop to all the false states of mind; staying in the realms of false thought, I don't apply comprehension, nor do I distinguish the real in this noncomprehension." This principle cannot be told to people: only those who have experienced enlightenment know what it really means as soon as it's mentioned.

37 The Inescapable

You report that since you received my letter, whenever you run into something inescapable amidst the hubbub, you've been examining yourself constantly, but without applying effort to meditate. This very inescapability itself is meditation: if you go further and apply effort to examine yourself, you're even further away. The old version of the Hua Yen says, "The Buddha Dharma is in daily activities, in walking, standing, sitting, and lying down, in eating and drinking, in talking and asking, in actions and conduct." And yet bestirring the mind isn't it. Right when you're in something inescapable, do not bestir your mind and think of examining yourself. The Ancestral Teacher said, "When discrimination doesn't arise, the light of emptiness shines by itself." Again, Layman P'ang said:

In daily activities without discrimination,
I alone naturally harmonize.
Not grasping or rejecting anywhere,
Not going with or going against.
Who considers crimson and purple honorable?
There's not a speck of dust in the mountains.
Spiritual powers and wondrous functioning:
Hauling water and carrying firewood.

Again, a former sage said, "There's only mental discrimination and calculation, the present awareness of one's own mind—it's all like a dream. Don't cling to it."

When you can't escape, you shouldn't exert your mind any further: when you don't exert your mind, everything appears. It doesn't matter whether your rational understanding is sharp or dull; it has nothing to do with matters of sharpness or dullness, nor does it have anything to do with quiet or confusion.

Just when you can't escape, suddenly you get rid of the cloth bag (of illusion) and without being aware of it you'll be clapping your hands and laughing loudly. Be sure to remember: if you employ the slightest effort to get realization of this affair, then you're like a person grasping empty space with his hands—it just helps you wear yourself out.

To Chang An-kuo

38   Contemplating a Saying

Before emotional consciousness has been smashed, the mind-fire burns bright. A just such a time, just take a saying you have doubts about to arouse and awaken yourself. For example: A monk asked Chao Chou, "Does a dog have Buddha-nature or not?" Chao Chou said, "No." Just bring this up to arouse and awaken yourself. Whatever side you come at it from, that's not it, you're wrong. Moreover, don't use mind to await enlightenment. And you shouldn't take up the saying in the citation of it. And you shouldn't understand it as the original subtlety, or discuss it as existent or nonexistent, or assess it as the nothingness of true nothingness. And you shouldn't sit in the bag of unconcern. And you shouldn't understand it in sparks struck from stone or in the brilliance of a lightning flash. There should be no place to employ your mind. When there's no place for mind, don't be afraid of falling into emptiness—on the contrary, this is a good place. Suddenly the rat enters a hollow ox horn,* and then wrong views are cut off.

This affair is neither difficult nor easy. Only if you have

---

* That is, discriminating consciousness reaches an impasse.

already planted deep the seeds of transcendent wisdom, and served men of knowledge through vast eons without beginning, and developed correct knowledge and correct views, does it strike you continuously in your present conduct as you meet situations and encounter circumstances in the midst of radiant spiritual consciousness, like recognizing your own parents in a crowd of people. At such a time, you don't have to ask anyone else: naturally the seeking mind does not scatter and run off.

Yun Men said, "When you can't speak, it's there; when you don't speak, it's not there. When you can't discuss it, it's there; when you don't discuss it, it's not there." He also commented saying, "You tell me, what is it when you're not discussing it?" Fearing people wouldn't understand, he also said, "What else is it?"

To Fu Li-shen

39 A Sudden Leap

Generally gentlemen who have been overly involved in worldly affairs for a long time have long been stuck like glue in the afflictions of the senses. When unexpectedly it happens that someone instructs them to do some meditation in a quiet place, and they temporarily get a feeling of unconcern, they immediately take this as the ultimate in peace and happiness. They are far from realizing that (quiescent unconcern) is like a rock pressing down on the grass. Though for a time they become aware that the scene is cut off, nevertheless the root and branches are still there: when will they experience quiescent extinction to the full? If you want to have real quiescent extinction appear before you, you must make a sudden leap within the fires of birth and death, and leap out without moving a hairsbreadth. Then you'll turn the rivers into pure ghee and the earth into gold; faced with situations, you'll be free to release or capture, to kill or bring life; no device to benefit others or benefit yourself will be impossible.

To Secretary Lou

40 Two Awakenings

In the old days the venerable Yen Yang asked Chao Chou, "What's it like when not bringing a single thing?" Chou said, "Put it down." Yen Yang said, "Since not a single thing is brought, put what down?" Chou said, "If you can't put it down, pick it up." At these words Yen Yang was greatly enlightened.

Again: a monk asked an ancient worthy, "What's it like when the student can't cope?" The ancient worthy said, "I too am like this." The monk said, "Teacher, why can't you cope either?" The ancient worthy said, "If I could cope, I could take away this inability to cope of yours." At these words the monk was greatly enlightened.

The enlightenment of these two monks is precisely where you are lost; where you have doubts is exactly where these two monks asked their questions. "Phenomena are born from discrimination, and also perish through discrimination. Wipe out all phenomena of discrimination—this Dharma has no birth or destruction."

41 Facing Death

You report that the last day of your life has already arrived. You should contemplate just like this in your daily activities— then the mind of worldly affliction will naturally come to an end. When the mind of affliction has come to an end, then the next day as before, early spring is still chilly. An ancient worthy said, "If you want to know the meaning of Buddha-nature, you must observe times and seasons, causes and conditions." This melting away of the mind of affliction is the time and season of Old Yellow Face (Buddha) appearing in the world and achieving buddhahood, the time and season of his sitting upon the Diamond Seat (of enlightenment), vanquishing armies of delusive demons, turning the Wheel of the Dharma, delivering sentient beings, and entering nirvana. It's no different from the time you've called "the last day of your life." To get here, just contemplate like this. This contemplation is called correct contemplation; contemplation different from this is called wrong contemplation. If you don't distinguish incorrect from correct, you won't avoid shifting and changing following after the times and seasons of others. If you want to get so you aren't following times and seasons, simply abandon it at once. Put it down where it can't be put down.

Don't take these words either. As before, it's just you, layman—there's no other man besides.

42 "There Is No Second Person"

Master Chang Ching said:

> The Ultimate Truth is wordless.
> People of the time do not realize this:
> They impose the practice of other things,
> Considering them accomplishments.
> They do not know that inherent nature has never been
>   sense objects,
> That it is the gate of subtle wondrous great liberation,
> Aware of all there is
> Without being stained or obstructed.
> This light has never stopped:
> From ages past up to the present
> It's been steady, never changing.
> Shining like the sun on near and far,
> Though it touches myriad colors,
> It doesn't mix with all of them.
> The subtle illumination of the spiritual light
> Does not depend on being cultivated and refined.
> Since they don't understand,
> People grasp the forms of things—
> It's just like rubbing the eyes.
> Falsely making optical illusions arise—
> They wear themselves out futilely,
> Passing many eons in vain.
> If you can turn back and reflect,
> There is no second person:
> All your conduct and activities
> Won't be lacking in the real aspect.

You say that you have dull faculties. Try to reflect back like this: see if the one who can recognize the dullness is dull too or not. If you don't turn the light around and reflect back, you're just keeping to your dull faculties and adding more affliction. That would be adding illusory falsehood to illusory falsehood, laying on optical illusion on top of optical illusion. Just listen: the one who can know that sense faculties are inherently dull is definitely not dull. Though you shouldn't hold to this dull one, you shouldn't abandon it to study, either; grasping and rejecting, sharp and dull—these have to do with people, not with Mind. This Mind is one substance with all the buddhas of the three worlds: there is no duality. If there were duality, the Dharma would not be of even sameness. "Receiving the teaching" and "transmitting Mind" are both empty falsehoods. Looking for truth and seeking reality seem even further off.

Just realize that Mind, with a single essence and no duality, definitely does not lie within sharp and dull or grasping and rejecting: then you'll see the moon and forget the finger, immediately making a clean break. If you linger further in thought, calculating before and after, then you're still understanding the empty fist as if it held something real, falsely concocting strange things amidst the phenomena of the sense objects, vainly confining yourself within matter, sensation, perception, volition, and consciousness, within the elements of sensory experience—you'll never get done.

43 It's Just You

I take it you have shut your gate and suspended your dealings with people, leaving aside all worldly affairs to arouse yourself day and night with the sayings I suggested to you. Very good, very good! In handling this mind, you must take enlightenment as the standard. If you shrink back saying your root nature is inferior, and then go on to seek an entry, this is truly "being inside the palace asking where the capital is." Right when you're arousing yourself, who is it? And who is it who knows your root nature is inferior? And who is it who is seeking an entry? Not avoiding the mouth-work, I'll explain it clearly for you layman: it's just you, Wang Yen-chang. There aren't two: there's only one Wang Yen-chang. Where else do we get the one who's arousing himself, the one who knows his root nature is inferior, the one who seeks an entry? You should know, they're all shadows of Wang Yen-chang. They have nothing to do with some other Wang Yen-chang. If it's the real Wang Yen-chang, then necessarily his root nature isn't inferior and he doesn't seek an entry. Just believe in yourself as your own master: it's not worth so much hassle.

In the old days there was a monk who asked Yang Shan, "In the Ch'an School's sudden enlightenment, what is the meaning of ultimate entry?" Yang Shan said, "The meaning of this is extremely difficult. Those in the School of the Ancestral Teachers with superior faculties and superior wisdom 'hear one, awaken to a thousand,' and attain total mental command. Even for people with these faculties, it's hard to understand (this meaning): how could people whose faculties are small and whose wisdom is meager get it? Therefore an ancient worthy said, 'If you don't meditate peacefully and still your thoughts, when you get here, you're always bound to be confused.'" The monk said, "Apart from this standard, are there any other expedients to enable students to gain entry or not?" Yang Shan said, "Whether or not there are any besides is making your mind uneasy. Now I ask you, where are you from?" The monk said, "From Yu Chou." Yang Shan said, "Do you still think of that place or not?" "I'm constantly thinking of it." Yang Shan said, "That place is filled with buildings and gardens and forests and people and horses. Think back to that which thinks: are there so many kinds there or not?" He said, "Here I don't see anything existing at all." Yang Shan said, "Your understanding is still in the objective—all right for the stage of faith, but not for your stage of personality." I've already been overly kind, but I must add a further note. "Stage of personality" means (you), Wang Yen-chang: "stage of faith" means the one who knows your root nature is inferior and who seeks an entry. Right when you're arousing yourself with a saying, reflect back: is the one that can do the arousing Wang Yen-chang or not? When you get here, there's not even room for a hair inside. If you linger in thought and hold back your potential, then you're being confused by shadows. Please apply your spirit soon—you shouldn't neglect this.

To Li Mao-chia

44 Who Is in the Way?

Your letter informs me that your root nature is dim and dull, so that though you make efforts to cultivate and uphold (the Dharma), you've never gotten an instant of transcendent enlightenment. The one who can recognize dim and dull is definitely not dim and dull: where else do you want to seek transcendent enlightenment? After all, gentlemen of affairs who study this Path must depend on their dimness and dullness to enter. But if you hold to dimness and dullness, considering yourself to be without the qualifications (for the Path), then you're being controlled by the demons of dimness and dullness. Since those with commonplace understanding often make the intention of seeking transcendent enlightenment into an obstacle set before them, their own correct understanding cannot appear before them. And this obstacle does not come from outside: it's nothing else but the boss-man who recognizes the dimness and dullness.

Thus when Master Jui Yen was dwelling constantly in his room, he would call to himself, "Boss!" and also respond to himself, "Yes?" "Be alert!" "I will." "Hereafter, don't fall for people's deceptions." "I won't." Fortunately since ancient times there've been such models!

Just arouse yourself right here, and see what it is. The one who does the arousing isn't anyone else, he's just the one that can recognize dimness and dullness. And the one who recognizes dimness and dullness isn't anyone else, he's your own fundamental identity. This is me giving medicine to suit the disease, having no other alternative; briefly pointing out the road for you to return home and sit in peace, and that's all. If you stick to dead words, and say it really is your fundamental identity, then you're acknowledging the conscious spirit as your self, and this has even less to do with it. Therefore Master Ch'ang Sha said, "People studying the Path don't know the truth: it's just because they've always accepted the conscious spirit. This, the root of birth and death over immeasurable ages, fools call the original man." What I said before about depending on dimness and dullness to enter is this. Simply see what the one who can know dimness and dullness like this ultimately is. Just look right here, don't seek transcendent enlightenment. Just observe and observe: suddenly you'll laugh aloud. Beyond this, there's nothing that can be said.

45 Meditation

Both torpor and excitation were condemned by the former sages. When you're sitting quietly, as soon as you feel the presence of either of these two diseases, just bring up the saying, "A dog has no Buddha-nature." Don't exert effort to push away these two kinds of disease—just be peaceful and still right there. Over a long time, as you become aware of saving power, this is the place where you gain power. Nor do you have to engage in quiet meditation—this itself is meditation.

46 Not "Keeping the Mind Still," but Mindlessness

Dear brother, if from the beginning you had never known of such matters as "keeping the mind still" and "forgetting concerns," then you would have found your nostrils wherever you touched. Though you may not fully know whether the teachers of the various localities are wrong or right, if your own basis is solid and genuine, the poisons of wrong doctrines will not be able to harm you, "keeping the mind still" and "forgetting concerns" included. If you always "forget concerns" and "keep the mind still," without smashing the mind of birth and death, then the delusive influences of form, sensation, perception, volition, and consciousness will get their way, and you'll inevitably be dividing emptiness into two. While quiet you experience immeasurable bliss; amidst clamor you experience immeasurable suffering. If you want to equalize bliss and suffering, don't arouse mind to "keep mind still," and don't use mind to "forget concerns"—twenty-four hours a day, let go and make yourself vast and expansive. When old habits suddenly arise, don't use mind to repress them; just go right to this sudden arising to observe a saying. "Does a dog have Buddha-nature or not? No." At just such a time, it's like a snowflake on a red-hot stove. For those with a discerning eye and a familiar hand, one leap and they leap clear. Only then do they know Lazy Jung's saying:

> Right when using mind,
> There's no mental activity.
> Crooked talk defiled with names and forms,
> Straight talk without complications.
> Without mind but functioning,
> Always functioning but nonexistent—
> The mindlessness I speak of now
> Is not separate from having mind.
> These aren't words to deceive people.

To Tsung Chih-ko

47 Contemplating "No"

You inform me that as you respond to circumstances in your daily involvement with differentiated objects, you're never not in the Buddha Dharma. You also say that amidst your daily activities and conduct you use the saying "A dog has no Buddha-nature" to clear away emotional defilements. If you make efforts like this, I'm afraid you'll never attain enlightened entry. Please examine what's under your feet: where do differentiated objects arise from? How can you smash emotional defilements in the midst of your activities with the saying "A dog has no Buddha-nature?" Who is it who can know he's clearing away emotional defilements?

Didn't Buddha say: "Sentient beings are inverted: they lose themselves and pursue things." Basically things have no inherent nature: those who lose themselves pursue them on their own. Originally objects are undifferentiated: those who lose themselves do their own differentiating. (You say) you have daily contact with differentiated objects, and you're also within the Buddha Dharma. If you're in the Buddha Dharma, it's not an object of differentiation; if you're among differentiated objects, then it's not the Buddha Dharma. Pick one up, let one go—what end will there be?

At the Nirvana Assembly,* the broad-browed butcher put down his slaughtering knife and immediately attained buddhahood where he stood. How could you have so much sadness and sorrow? In your daily activities as you respond to circumstances, as soon as you become aware of being involved with differentiated objects, just go to the differentiating to raise the saying "A dog has no Buddha-nature." Don't think of it as clearing away, and don't think of it as emotional defilement; don't think of it as differentiation, and don't think of it as the Buddha Dharma—simply contemplate the saying "A dog has no Buddha-nature." Just bring up the word "No." And don't set your mind on it and await enlightenment. If you do, objects and the Buddha Dharma are differentiated, emotional defilements and the saying "A dog has no Buddha-nature" are differentiated, interrupted and uninterrupted are differentiated,

---

* The Nirvana Assembly: the day and night before Buddha passed on, when he expounded the *Nirvana Scripture.*

and encountering the confusion of emotional defilements so body and mind are unsettled and being able to know so many differentiations are also differentiated.

If you want to remove this disease, just contemplate the word "No." Just look at the broad-browed butcher putting down his knife and saying, "I am one of the thousand Buddhas." True or false? If you assess it as false or true, again you plunge into objects of differentiation. It's not as good as cutting it in two with a single stroke. Don't think of before and after: if you think of before and after, this is more differentiating.

Hsuan Sha said this matter "Cannot be limited—the road of thought is cut off. It does not depend on an array of adornments—from the beginning it's been real and pure. Moving, acting, talking, laughing, clearly understanding wherever you are, there's nothing more lacking. People these days do not understand the truth in this, and vainly involve themselves with sensory phenomena, getting defiled all over and tied down everywhere. Even if they understand, sense objects are present in complex confusion, names and forms are not genuine, so they try to freeze their minds and gather in their attention, taking things and returning them to emptiness, shutting their eyes, hiding their eyes; if a thought starts up, they immediately demolish it; as soon as the slightest conception arises, they immediately press it down. Those with a view like this are outsiders who have fallen into empty annihilation, dead men whose spirits have not yet departed, dark and silent, without awareness or knowledge. They're 'covering their ears to steal the bell,' vainly deluding themselves."

All you said in your letter was the disease Hsuan Sha condemned—the perverted Ch'an of quiescent illumination, a pit to bury people in. You must realize this. When you bring up a saying, don't use so many maneuvers at all—just don't let there be any interruption whether you're walking, standing, sitting, or lying down. Don't discriminate joy and anger, sorrow and bliss. Just keep on bringing up the saying, raising it and raising it, looking and looking. When you feel there's no road for reason and no flavor, and in your mind you're oppressed and troubled, this is the place for each person to abandon his body and his life. Remember, don't shrink back in your mind when you see a realm like this—such a realm is precisely the scene for becoming a buddha and being an ancestral teacher.

And yet the false teachers of silent illumination just consider wordlessness as the ultimate principle, calling it the matter of "the Other Side of the Primordial Buddha," or of "before the Empty Eon." They don't believe there is a gate of enlightenment, and consider enlightenment as a lie, as something secondary, as an expedient word, as an expression to draw people in. This crowd deceive others and deceive themselves, lead others into error and go wrong themselves. You should also realize this.

In the conduct of your daily activities, as you're involved with differentiated objects, when you become aware of saving power, this is where you gain power. Gaining power is the ultimate in saving power. If you use the slightest power to uphold it, this is definitely a false method—it's not Buddhism. Just take the mind, so long-lasting, and bring it together with the saying "A dog has no Buddha-nature." Keep them together till the mind has no place to go—suddenly, it's like awakening from a dream, like a lotus flower opening, like parting the clouds and seeing the moon. When you reach such a moment, naturally you attain unity. Through the upsets and errors of your daily activities, just contemplate the word "No." Don't be concerned with awakening or not awakening, getting through or not getting through. All the Buddhas of the three worlds were just unconcerned people, people for whom there is nothing; all the generations of ancestral teachers too were just people without concerns. An ancient worthy said, "Just comprehend nothingness in the midst of things, unconcern amidst concerns: when seeing forms and hearing sounds, don't act blind and deaf." Another ancient worthy said, "Fools remove objects but don't obliterate mind; the wise wipe out mind without removing objects." Since in all places there's no mind, all kinds of objects of differentiation are nonexistent of themselves.

Gentlemen of affairs these days, though, are quick to want to understand Ch'an. They think a lot about the scriptural teachings and the sayings of the ancestral teachers, wanting to be able to explain clearly. They are far from knowing that this clarity is nonetheless an unclear matter. If you can penetrate the word "No," you won't have to ask anyone else about clear and unclear. I teach gentlemen of affairs to let go and make themselves dull—this is this same principle. And it's not bad to get first prize in looking dull, either—I'm just afraid you'll hand in an empty paper. What a laugh!

To Huang Po-ch'eng

48   Abandon Them at Once

It's a great error to know you are deluded and not awaken. To cling to delusion and wait for awakening is also a big mistake. Why? You're deluded because you don't awaken: to hold to delusion and wait for enlightenment is to be even more unaware, even more deluded. If you want to smash these two heavy barriers, please abandon them at once. If you can't abandon them, how can there ever be a stop to delusion after delusion, awakening after awakening?

To Tseng T'ien-yu

49 "Don't Keep Knowledge"

When you study this Path, before you've gained an entry, it feels endlessly difficult. When you hear the comments of the teachers of the school, it seems even harder to understand. This is because if the mind that grasps for realization and seeks rest is not removed, you are obstructed by this. As soon as this mind stops, you finally realize that the Path is neither difficult nor easy, and also that it cannot be passed on by teachers.

If you want to use mind to await enlightenment and rest, even if you study from where you stand now until Maitreya is born, you still won't be able to attain enlightenment or rest: you'll be increasing your delusion and unhappiness. Master P'ing T'ien said,

Spiritual light undimmed,
The excellent advice of the ages:
To enter this gate,
Don't keep knowledge.

Another ancient worthy said, "This Matter cannot be sought with mind and cannot be attained without mind; it can't be told with words and it can't be conveyed with silence." This is first-class trailing mud and dripping water, extremely compassionate talk. Often people studying the Path just read past these pointers like this, without examining them carefully to see what principle this is. If you're a man with bones and sinews, as soon as you hear this mentioned, you immediately take the Diamond King's jewel sword and with one blow cut off these four roads of complications—thus the road of birth and death is cut off, the road of ordinary and holy is cut off, the road of calculation and thought is cut off, and the road of gain and loss, of right and wrong, is cut off too. Right where the person stands, he's purified and clean, naked and free, and ungraspable—won't he be happy and content?

Haven't you read of Master Kuan Hsi's first encounter with Lin Chi in the old days? When Lin Chi saw him coming he got down off his meditation bench and abruptly held him tightly to his breast. Kuan Hsi immediately said, "I get it, I get it!" Lin Chi knew he had already penetrated, so he immediately pushed him away and had no more words to discuss with him. At such a time, how could Kuan Hsi think or calculate or reply? Fortunately since ancient times there have been models like this, but people these days, because of their crude minds, don't make it their business. If from the first Kuan Hsi had had the least intention of waiting for enlightenment, realization, or rest, don't tell me he would have been immediately enlightened when he was held fast. No, then he would have been dragged around the world with his hands and feet bound, unable to gain either enlightenment or rest.

50 Knowledge as a Barrier and as a Companion

You tell me that you've had faith in this Path since your early years, but in later years you've been obstructed by your knowledge and understanding, and have never had an enlightened entry. You want to know an expedient method for fully comprehending the Path day and night—since we're being perfectly conscientious, I wouldn't presume to judge the case from outside, but a few creeping vines may be permitted:

This very one seeking enlightenment and entry has been the knowledge and understanding that obstructs the Path. What other knowledge is there to obstruct you? Ultimately, what is being called knowledge? Where does the knowledge come from? And who is being obstructed? In this one statement of yours, there are three mistakes: saying you are obstructed by knowledge is one, saying you are not yet enlightened, and willingly being deluded is another, and going on within delusion to use mind to wait for enlightenment is another. These three mistakes are the root of birth and death. You must stop producing them for a moment, so the mind of these errors is cut off: only then do you realize that there is no delusion to be smashed, no enlightenment to be expected, and no knowledge that can cause obstruction. You'll be like a man drinking water, who knows for himself whether it is cold or warm. After a long time, naturally you won't entertain this view.

Just go to the mind that can know knowledge to see if it too can cause obstruction, to see if in the mind that can know knowledge there are so many kinds or not. Since ancient times, people with great wisdom have all taken knowledge as their companion, considered knowledge an expedient means, practiced the compassion of equanimity in knowledge, and done all the business of buddhas in knowledge, like dragons reaching the water, like tigers taking to the mountains—they never considered this knowledge an affliction, because they thoroughly understood the origin of knowledge. Once you recognize the origin of knowledge, then this very knowledge is a field of liberation, the place to get out of birth and death. Since it's the site of liberation, the place to escape birth and death, the knower is quiescent and extinct in his own essential being. Since the knower is quiescent and extinct, the one who can know knowledge cannot but be quiescent and extinct. Enlightenment and Nirvana, True Thusness and Buddha-nature cannot but be quiescent and extinct. What else is there that can cause obstruction? Where else will you seek enlightenment and entry?

To the Ch'an man Miao Tao

51 One Path Pure and Even

You, Miao Tao, "Great Master of the Light of Concentration," asked me "Please point out the concise essentials of this mind and this inherent nature, of delusion and enlightenment, of turning towards and turning away." I was silent and didn't answer. When you asked again, I laughed and said, "As for the concise essentials, they cannot be pointed out to people. If it could be pointed out, it wouldn't be the essentials." You said, "How can you have no expedient means to enable me to go towards (the Path)?" I said, "As for expedients, well then: with mind, there's no delusion or enlightenment; with inherent nature, there's no turning towards or turning away."

But people set up views of delusion and enlightenment and hold to interpretations of turning towards and turning away, wanting to understand this mind and see this inherent nature; thus this mind and this nature immediately flow into wrong paths, following the person's inversions, errors, and confusion. Hence enlightenment is not distinguished from delusion, nor the wrong separated from the correct. Because they do not fully understand the dreamlike illusion of "this mind" and "this nature," they falsely establish pairs of terms: they consider turning towards and turning away, delusion and enlightenment, as real, and accept this mind and this nature as true. They are far from realizing that whether true or not true, false or not false, worldly or world-transcending, these are merely provisional statements.

Thus Vimalakirti said, "The Dharma cannot be seen, heard, perceived, or known. If you employ seeing, hearing, perceiving, and knowing, then this is seeing, hearing, perceiving, and knowing—it's not seeking the Dharma."

Another ancient worthy said, "If you grasp your own self and your own mind as the ultimate, there must be other things and other people to be the opposite."

Again, Buddha told "The Kindly One" (foremost among his chief disciples in expounding the Dharma): "You use the characteristics of form and void to overturn and eliminate each other in the Repository of Thusness, which accordingly becomes form or void and extends through the cosmos. I use subtle illumination undestroyed and unborn, to merge with the Repository of Thusness, so the Repository of Thusness is nothing but the light of subtle awakening shining throughout the cosmos." So Buddha was provisionally indicating that using form and void to overturn and eliminate each other is wrong, and considering subtle illumination undestroyed and unborn as right. These are medicinal words, to cure the two diseases, delusion and enlightenment, not a set definition by the Buddha: words to smash the clinging to delusion and enlightenment, mind and nature, turning towards and turning away, as real things. Haven't you read, the Bodhisattva of the Diamond Treasury said, "All the three worlds are only verbal statements. All the various phenomena have no basis in verbal statements, and all verbal statements have no basis within all the various phenomena."

If views of delusion and enlightenment perish and interpretations of turning towards and turning away are cut off, then this mind is lucid and clear as the bright sun and this nature is vast and open as empty space; right where the person stands, he emits light and moves the earth, shining through the ten directions. Those who see this light all realize acceptance of things as unborn. When you arrive at such a time, naturally you are in tacit accord with this mind and this nature. Only then do you know that in the past there was basically no delusion and now there is basically no enlightenment, that enlightenment is delusion and delusion is enlightenment, that turning towards and turning away are identical, that inherent nature is identical to mind and mind is identical to inherent nature, that buddhas are delusive demons and delusive demons are buddhas, that the One Path is pure and even, that there is no equal or not equal—all this will be the constant lot of one's own mind, not dependent on the skills of another.

Even so, it's from lack of any other choice again that I say this: don't immediately consider this as really true. If you consider it really true, then you're ignorant of expedient means, accepting dead words as fixed, multiplying empty falsehoods, producing even more confusion—there will be no end to it.

When you get here, where there's no way to use your mind, it's not as good as knowing of such things, but putting them to one side, and turning to the Great Master Ma's "Mind itself is Buddha," and "Not mind, not Buddha," and "It's not mind, it's not Buddha, it's not things"; or Chao Chou's (answer to "What is the meaning of the coming from the west?") "The cypress tree in the garden"; or Yun Men's (answer to "When not giving rise to a single thought, is there fault or not?") "Mt. Sumeru"; or Ta Yu's "Sawing apart the scale beam"; or Yun Yang's (answer to "What is Buddha?") "A lump of earth"; or Wu Ye of Fen Yang's (frequent reply to questioners) "Don't think falsely"; or Chu T'i's (lifelong teaching by simply) raising a finger—ultimately, what principle is it? This, then, is my expedient means. Think it over, Miao Tao.

To Fan Mao-shih

52 Buddhism and Ch'an Talk

You say you can practice Buddhism, but don't understand Ch'an talk. Being able and not being able are neither different nor the same. Just realize that being able to practice is identical to Ch'an words. To understand Ch'an words but be unable to practice Buddhism is like a man sitting in water complaining of thirst, or sitting in food complaining of hunger—what's the difference? You must realize that Ch'an words are the business of buddhas and the business of buddhas is identical to Ch'an words. Being able to understand, being able to practice—this has to do with people, not with the Dharma.

53 One Suchness

To take up This Great Affair, you must have a determined will. If you're half believing and half in doubt, there'll be no connection. An ancient worthy said, "Studying the Path is like drilling for fire. You still can't stop when you get smoke: Only when sparks appear is the return home complete." Want to know where it's complete? It's the worlds of self and the worlds of others as One Suchness.*

54 Cut It Off Directly

Master Chao Chou said, "For twenty years, except for the two mealtimes of gruel and rice which were mixed application of mind, I've had no other points of mixed use of mind. This is how I really act." Don't understand it as the Buddha Dharma or the Ch'an Path. Impermanence is swift, the matter of birth and death important. In the world of sentient beings things

---

* When their real nature is seen, all phenomena are Thus, all are One Suchness. Yen Shou quotes the scriptures. The Diamond Sutra: "Since 'thus' (or 'so' or 'such') is taken as 'enlightened,' all phenomena are Thus—what thing isn't So? If one believes in One Suchness, this is awakening to the basic reality, producing definitive release, entering the gate of independent mastery." The Hua Yen: "When outside of knowledge there is no suchness which is entered by knowledge, and outside of suchness there is no knowledge which acts to realize suchness, then mind and objects are Thus, and the One Path is pure."

which go along with birth and death are (numerous) as hemp or millet—every time you've disposed of them properly, they come back again. If you don't stick the words "birth and death" on the tip of your nose as a countermeasure, then when the last day of your life arrives, your limbs will be in panic and confusion, like a crab dropped in boiling water—then you'll finally know repentance, but too late. If you want to be direct, then cut it off immediately starting right now.

To Teng Tzu-li

55   Faith

If you want to study this Path, you must have settled faith, so your mind does not waver whether favorable or adverse environments are encountered—only then do you have some direction in the Path. Buddha said, "Faith can forever destroy the root of affliction; faith can focus you on the virtues of buddhahood. Faith has no attachments to objects; far removed from all difficulties, you get so there is no difficulty." He also said, "Faith can transcend the numerous roads of delusion, and display the Path of unexcelled liberation."

In the Teachings there are clear passages like the above: how could Buddha deceive people? If you're half light and half dark, half believing and half not believing, then whenever you meet with situations and encounter circumstances, your mind produces doubt and confusion—this is mind having attachments to objects. Not being able to be definite and have no doubts about this Path, to destroy the root of affliction and get away from all difficulty, is entirely due to lack of settled faith, to being confused by the delusions of one's own personal existence. If you can be birthless for a moment amidst causal origination, then without going beyond this moment you instantly transcend the roads of delusion. What are being called "roads of delusion" are nothing else but dimming this mind: outside this mind you falsely produce all differentiated views, so this mind immediately flows along after the false differentiating thoughts, thus forming objects of delusion. If you can believe directly that this mind has definitely attained enlightenment from the beginning, and abruptly forget all your views, then these roads of delusion themselves are the route of enlightenment by which the person escapes from birth and death.

To Tseng T'ien-yu

56   Returning to *Prajna*

The Taoists with their false concepts and ideas all think of imbibing the light of the sun and moon, swallowing mists and taking vapors. Even if they could stay in the world keeping their physical forms without being afflicted by cold or heat, how could they wholly return this mind and this thought into the midst of *prajna*? A former sage clearly said, "It's like a moth: it can land anywhere, only it can't land on the flames of a fire. The mind of sentient beings is also thus: it can become attached anywhere, only it can't become attached to *prajna*." If from moment to moment you don't retreat from your first aspiration, but take your own mind and consciousness that are attached to the worldly, to sensory afflictions, and bring them back onto *prajna,* then although you don't penetrate in this lifetime, when faced with the end of your life, you definitely won't be dragged into evil paths (to be reborn less than human) by evil deeds. In a lifetime to come you will appear according to the power of your aspiration in your present life, and surely receive the use of it spontaneously within *prajna*. This is something definite, without a doubt.

To Cheng, an Imperial official

57 Two Roads

When the last day of your life arrives, neither love nor power nor riches nor innate spirit nor official position nor wealth and rank will be of any use. When the vision fails, there are only the realms of two paths that appear, one and one—the paths of doing good and doing evil during your life. If you've done much evil and little good, then you're swept away according to your evil deeds. If you've done much good and little evil, then you are born according to your good deeds as a deva or human, in the house of the ten virtues. Once you know that these two roads are both in the province of empty illusion, then you generate a mind firm and unflinching, zealous and vigorously advancing, to transcend feelings and detach from views and penetrate through and out of birth and death. Then, on the last day of your life, the two roads, good and evil, will not be able to hold you.

58 Release

You report that since you got back to the city, where you wear clothes and eat food and enjoy your family, where everything is as before, since you've lost the feeling of being tied down and aren't thinking of it as extraordinary, the former obstructions of your old habits have diminished and become slight—again and again you say you're leaping with joy. This is the result of studying Buddhism. If you are not great beyond measure, understanding a hundred and handling a thousand properly in a single laugh, then you cannot know that in our family there is indeed a subtle marvel not transmitted. Otherwise you'll never be able to destroy the two words "doubt" and "wrath" till the end of time. It wouldn't help even if the sky became my mouth and grass, trees, pebbles, and stones all emitted light to help me expound the truth. Thus we believe that this thing cannot be transmitted and cannot be studied: it requires one's own realization and enlightenment, one's own approval and stopping: only then does one reach the end. Your one laugh right now abruptly obliterates attainment—what else is there to say?

Old Yellow Face (Buddha) said, "I don't cling to what sentient beings say—it's all conditioned phenomena, empty and false. Though I don't depend on words to speak, I also don't use wordlessness to preach." What you said in your letter, that you've lost the feeling of constraint and haven't been entertaining thoughts of the extraordinary, tacitly accords with what Old Yellow Face said. What's identical to this talk is called enlightened talk; what's apart from it is called deluded talk. My whole life I've had a great vow that I'd rather suffer the pains of hell with this body on behalf of all sentient beings, than portray the Buddha Dharma with this mouth as a human sentiment, and blind people's eyes.

Since you've gotten to this stage, and know for yourself that this thing is not obtained from others, just go on as before for a while—no need to ask any more if you understand the Great Dharma or not, or if you are obstructed or not as you respond to potentialities. If you entertain such notions, then you're not as before.

I take it that after the summer you can come back out here. This pleases me very much. If you were still so eager, frantically seeking without respite, then this wouldn't do.

Seeing the great extent of your joy the last few days, I didn't presume to comment, fearing my words would give offense. Now that your joy has settled, I'll dare to point something out. With this affair, it's extremely important that you don't take it easy: to get it right, you must feel shame. Frequently those with sharp faculties and superior wisdom attain it without expending a lot of effort, so they think of taking it easy, and therefore don't cultivate it. Many are carried off by the objects before them, so they cannot be the master. As days and months pass, they're deluded and don't turn back. Since their power in the Path cannot subdue the power of their actions, delusion gets its way—they're sure to be controlled by delusive demons. When faced with the end of their lives, they won't have gained power.

Be sure to remember the words of a previous day: "In principle, it's sudden enlightenment; taking advantage of enlightenment to clear everything away. In the event, phenomena are not suddenly removed, but exhausted gradually." Whether you're walking, standing, sitting, or lying down, you must not forget! As for all the different kinds of sayings of the ancients, don't consider them true and don't consider them false. Over a long time as you become completely ripe, naturally you will reach silent accord with your own fundamental mind; you don't have to seek special excellence or extraordinary wonders besides.

Master Shui Lao asked Ma Tsu, "What is the true meaning of the coming from the West?" Ma Tsu then knocked him down with a kick to the chest: Shui Lao was greatly enlightened. He got up clapping his hands and laughing loudly and said, "How extraordinary! How wonderful! Instantly, on the tip of a hair, I've understood the root source of myriad states of concentration and countless subtle meanings." Then he bowed and withdrew. Afterwards, he would tell the assembly, "From the time I took Ma Tsu's kick up until now, I haven't stopped laughing."

One day Ku Shan approached Hsueh Feng. Feng knew his circumstances were ripe, so he suddenly got up, held him tight, and said, "What is it?" Opening up, Ku Shan was completely enlightened—he even forgot his comprehending mind and just raised his hand and waved, nothing more. Feng said, "Will you express some principle?" Ku Shan said, "How could there be any principle?"

Having left the Fifth Ancestral Teacher's place, Hui Neng traveled south for two months, and had reached the Ta Yu Range (that divides Kiangsi from Kwangtung). He was pursued by the monk Hui Ming, who was originally a general, accompanied by several hundred men, who wanted to seize the robe and bowl (emblematic of succession to the ancestral teachers). Ming was the first to overtake him. The Sixth Ancestral Teacher threw down the robe and bowl on a rock and said, "This robe signifies faith: how can it be taken by force?" Ming tried to pick up the robe and bowl, but was unable to move them. At that point he said, "I have come for the Dharma, not for the robe." The Ancestral Teacher said, "Since you've come for the Dharma, you should put to rest all your motivations, and don't give rise to a single thought, and I will explain for you." After a silence, he said, "Without thinking of good, and without thinking of evil, at just such a time, which is your original face?" At these words Hui Ming was greatly enlightened. He also asked, "Besides the intimate words and meaning that struck home of a moment ago, is there any further intimate message?" The Ancestral Teacher said, "If it were said to you, it wouldn't be intimate. If you turn around and reflect, what's intimate is in you." Ming said, "Though I was at Huang Mei (the Fifth Ancestral Teacher's place), I never really had insight into my own face. Now encountering your instruction, I am like a man drinking water who knows for himself whether it's cold or warm. Now you are my teacher, layman."

Comparing the release in your one laugh with the cases of the three venerable adepts, which is better, which is worse? Please decide for yourself. Are there any more extraordinary principles besides? If there are, then apparently you were never released and opened up.

"Just know how to be a buddha: don't worry that a buddha won't know how to talk." Since ancient times, people who have attained the Path, since they are full themselves, have put forth their own surplus to respond to potentials and receive beings. They are like a bright mirror on its stand, like a bright jewel in the palm of the hand: when an outsider comes an outsider appears, and when a native comes a native appears. And it's not intentional: if it were intentional, then there would be a real doctrine to give to people. You want to be clear about the Great Dharma, to respond to people's potentials without getting stuck. Simply go on as before for a while: no need to ask anyone else, just go on checking yourself for a long long time.

As for words to report your current situation, please make a note to yourself, and don't say anything beyond this: for the state you're in they'd all be superfluous words. Like trailing vines, the verbal complications would be too numerous; stop doing this for a while.

59   An Ordinary Fellow Who Understands Things

Recently it's been hot and humid. I wonder whether or not, in your retreat, you've been relaxed and open and naturally so, without being disturbed by all the demons of delusion; whether or not, within your daily activities and conduct, you've become one with the saying "A dog has no Buddha-nature"; whether or not you are able to make no distinction between motion and stillness; whether or not you've merged dreaming and wakefulness; whether or not you've joined inner truth and phenomena; whether or not (for you) mind and objects are all Thus. Old P'ang said,

> Mind is Thus and objects are also Thus:
> There is no true and also no false.
> Existence doesn't concern me,
> Nor does nonexistence hold me:
> I'm not a holy sage,
> But an ordinary fellow who understands things.

If you can truly be an ordinary fellow who's understood things, then what mudballs are Shakyamuni and Bodhidharma, what a warm bowl of noise are the teachings of the canon of the Three Vehicles!

When you have your own faith without doubts in this method—and it's no small matter—you must make the raw ripe and make the stale fresh to begin to have a small share of Accord with This Matter. Gentlemen of affairs often get a glimpse in the unexpected, but lose it when things are as intended. I must let you know: when things are going according to your ideas you must always be mindful of the times when they don't follow your intentions—don't forget even for a moment!

"Just get the root, don't worry about the branches. Just know how to be a buddha, don't worry that a buddha won't know how to talk." This one is easy to get but hard to keep. Don't neglect it! You must make yourself correct from head to tail, extending and fulfilling it. Then afterwards you put forth your own surplus to reach other beings.

To Master Kuei

60   How to Teach

Now that you've obtained outside support, you're thinking that you can put aside human affairs and do Buddhist things all the time with patchrobed monks. Over a long time, as you become especially excellent, you can expect furthermore to conduct detailed examinations with them in your room. You must not tolerate human feelings, or fall into the weeds with them. Instruct them directly with your own provisions, and teach them to awaken and attain for themselves: only then will it be the way venerable adepts help others. If you see them lingering in doubt without comprehending, and so you add footnotes for them, not only do you blind their eyes, but also you lose the proper method of your own family.

61 Be Thoroughgoing

Now that you have taken up This Affair, you must steadfastly make yourself thoroughgoing, and sit upright in a room with what you've truly experienced and awakened to in the course of your life. It's like crossing a bridge made of a single plank carrying a two-hundred-pound burden: if your hands and feet slip, you can't even preserve your own life, much less save others. An ancient worthy said, "This Affair is like an old man of eighty taking the stage: how could it be child's play?" Another ancient worthy said, "If I propagated the teaching of the school the same way all the time, the weeds in front of the dharma hall would be ten feet deep. Better have someone check the courtyard." When monks came seeking the Path, Mu Chou would say, "An obvious case: I forgive you thirty blows." Wu Ye of Fen Yang told questioners, "No false thinking!" Whenever Lu Tsu saw a monk enter the gate, he would immediately turn around and sit facing the wall. When helping others, you must not dim this style: only then do you not lose the meaning of this school which has come down from antiquity.

62 Models of Teaching

When patchrobed ones come into the teacher's room, he must cut to the crux—he shouldn't slog through mud and water. For example, when Ch'an Master K'ung of Hsueh Feng was with Yun Chu and Yun Men, the moment they got together the old fellows knew that K'ung wasn't fooling himself, that he was a man of the Buddha Dharma. Therefore, they taught him with "one flavor," using their own proper hammer and tongs. Later in another place, K'ung's mastery was unfurled: when he'd understood the Great Dharma, he at once acquired the use of the hammer and tongs that he had received, and finally knew.

I don't consider the Buddha Dharma to be a human sentiment. Last year I sent a booklet of remarks, which, though hurried, don't lose the message of Lin Chi's School. Now I'm sending it to their quarters for the patchrobed ones to read. I took up brush to write especially to propagate the teaching, to serve legitimate patchrobed ones as a model for expounding the Dharma in the future. If in the beginning I had dragged through the mud and water for them, preaching old lady Ch'an, later, after their eyes opened, they'd be sure to scold me, without a doubt. Therefore an ancient said, "I don't esteem my late teacher's virtues in the Path: I just honor the way he didn't explain it all for me. If he had explained it all for me, how could there be Today?"* This is the same principle.

Chao Chou said, "If you tell me to receive people according to their potentials, the twelve-part teaching of the three vehicles has already received them. Here at my place, I just use my own thing to receive people. If I can't, it's that the student's root nature is slow and dull—it's none of my affair." Think about it!

---

* Today, the day of enlightenment. Lin Chi said, "Today, a man of power finally knows that fundamentally there is nothing; basically there are no concerns. It's because you can't fully believe this that you go from minute to minute frantically seeking, abandoning a head to look for a head, unable to stop yourself. . . . According to the understanding of the Ch'an School, it's not this way—it's simply right now, the present: there is no other time. All that I say is matching medicines to the diseases of a certain era—there's no real doctrine whatsoever. . . ."

Those who study words often say that Kuei Tsung cutting the snake and Nan Ch'uan killing the cat* are "taking charge of the situation with subtle action"; they call it "the Great Function being manifested without keeping to rules." Thus they don't realize that it's not this kind of principle at all. If you have the transcendental eye, then you know what it means as soon as its mentioned. If you don't understand the Great Dharma, and just play games, when will there be an end to it?

---

* Two well-known stories:

A lecturer-monk had come to see Kuei Tsung, who happened to be chopping weeds. As Kuei Tsung was chopping with his hoe, a snake suddenly appeared: Kuei Tsung immediately killed it with a chop of his hoe. The lecturer said, "I have long heard of Kuei Tsung, but now that I've come here, he's actually a crude-acting monk." Kuei Tsung said, "Is it you or I who's crude?" The lecturer said, "What is crude and coarse?" Kuei Tsung held the hoe upright. "What is subtle and fine?" Kuei Tsung made the motion of chopping. The lecturer said, "If so, then you act according to it." Kuei Tsung said, "Leaving aside acting according to it for a minute, where did you see me cutting the snake?" The lecturer was speechless.

Nan Ch'uan appeared as the monks of the eastern and western halls were fighting over a cat. He told them, "If you can speak, then you'll save the cat. If you cannot say anything, I'll kill it." There was no reply from the crowd, so Nan Ch'uan killed the cat.

When Chao Chou returned, Nan Ch'uan told him what he'd said before. Chao Chou immediately took off his shoes, put them on top of his head, and left. Nan Ch'uan said, "If you'd been here before, you would have saved the cat."

63   Where Is Home?

In the old days, Layman P'ang said:

I have a boy who hasn't married,
I have a girl who hasn't been married—
The whole family gathers round,
And together we talk of birthlessness.

Later on there was a layman called the "Non-doing Layman," surnamed Yang. He had studied with the former generation (of Ch'an masters) and had real empowerment in our school. To this verse of Layman P'ang's he once said:

When a boy grows up he should marry,
When a girl matures she should be married off—
What leisure time do they seek,
To go on talking of birthlessness?

These two laymen didn't seek "official" approval for their stage of universal, everlasting oneness: each set his own boundaries, saying "I know it exists," and where there are no buddhas, always proclaimed himself the honored one.*

At that time there was another uncommon one: he was called the Ch'an Master of Ocean Seal Faith, and lived at the time in Su Chou's Ting Hui Temple. On seeing this verse of the Non-doing Layman, he too had a verse which said:

I have no boy to get married,
And no girl to marry off—
When tired I sleep:
Why be concerned with talk of birthlessness?

---

* At birth Shakyamuni Buddha is said to have proclaimed, "In heaven and on earth, I alone am the honored one."

You see these three old fellows saying these three verses with your eyes open, with them closed, and with them neither open nor closed. I can see them: looking on them impartially, they're not nonexistent. Ultimately, do you see them with your eyes open, with your eyes closed, or with them neither open nor closed? If you see them with your eyes open, then you fall into Layman P'ang's trap; if you see them with your eyes closed, then you fall into "Non-doing" Yang's trap; if you see them with eyes neither open nor closed, then you fall into the Ocean Seal Ch'an Master's trap. Seeing me talk like this, you're sure to say, "Not any of those ways." If it's not any of those ways, you still fall into my trap. To escape the traps of the three elders is easy: to get out of my trap is hard. Ultimately, how will you get out? When you get back to Yen Ping, after you've married off your daughter, I explain it all for you at length.

Since I've remembered another verse by an ancient worthy, I'll add it at the end—I hope you won't get hung up on it. Then too, it's out of my excessive kindness (that I add this). The verse says:

Studying the Path is like drilling for fire:
When you get smoke, you can't stop yet;
Only when sparks appear,
Is the return home accomplished.

I have one more question: where is the home you return to, K'uai-jan? If you can penetrate this question, boys marrying and girls marrying are both within it. If you don't know the home, then your karmic consciousness is dim and confused, and if you're always running around on the outside, it wouldn't surprise me.

64   Attainment from Causal Circumstances

In the old days Master Ling Yun suddenly awakened to the
Path on seeing peach blossoms. He had a verse which said,

> For thirty years I sought a master swordsman:
> How many times the leaves fell and shoots sprouted!
> Ever since I once saw peach blossoms,
> Up to right now, no more doubts.

The Master Kuei Shan investigated his enlightenment and gave
him his seal; as he was approving him he said, "When you
awaken to the Path from causal circumstances, there's never
any retrogression."

Then again, when the Master Hsueh Feng wrote his own
epitaph he said:

> If you attain from causal circumstances,
> It begins and ends, forms and disintegrates.
> If it's not from causal circumstances that you attain,
> It endures through the ages, everlasting and solid.

Tell me, are the viewpoints of these two venerable adepts
the same or different? If you say they're the same, one man
considers attainment from causal conditions right and one
man considers it wrong. If you say they're different, it's impossible that the two great elders were setting up divergent sects
to confuse later people with doubts. If you don't understand,
I'll explain it for you directly:

> Two exist because of one—
> Don't even keep the one!
> When the one man isn't born
> The myriad phenomena are without fault.

The difference between the two previous verse passages is resolved in the above verse. Bah!

To Tseng T'ien-yu

65   Dream and Reality

I take it you dreamed of burning incense and entering my room. How relaxed and easy! Don't interpret this as a dream: you must realize it was real room-entering. Haven't you read how Shariputra asked Subhuti, "To expound the six transcendences (*paramitas*) in a dream, to expound the six transcendences while awake—are these the same or different?" Subhuti said, "The meaning of this is profound—I can't explain it. The Great Being Maitreya is here at this assembly: go to him and ask." Bah! Not a little overindulgent. Hsueh Tou said, "At that time, if he hadn't let him go, but had followed up giving him a thrust—'Who says Maitreya?' 'Who is Maitreya?'—then we would have seen the ice melted and the tiles scattered." Bah! Hsueh Tou too is quite overindulgent.

If someone asked, "When the Retired Military Governor Tseng dreamed he entered your room, was this the same or different from (entering) when awake?" I'd immediately say to him, "Who is the room-enterer? What is 'entering the room'? Who is dreaming? Who is it that speaks of the dream? Who is it that doesn't interpret it as a dream? Who is the real room-enterer?" Bah! This too is rather overindulgent.

66 Real Merit

Emperor Wu of Liang asked Bodhidharma, "I have built temples and had monks ordained without number: what merit is there in this?" Bodhidharma said, "There is no merit." The Emperor said, "Why no merit?" Bodhidharma said, "These are just the lesser fruits of gods and men, causes of defilement; like shadows following shapes, though they're there, they're not real." The Emperor said, "What is true merit?" Bodhidharma answered, "The subtle perfection of pure wisdom, its essence naturally empty and still. Such merit is not to be sought with worldly means." Only then did the Emperor ask, "What is the highest meaning of the holy truths?" Bodhidharma answered, "Empty, without holiness." The Emperor said, "Who is facing me?" Bodhidharma replied, "I don't know." The Emperor did not understand, so Bodhidharma crossed the river into Wei. If you want to see real merit right now, don't look for it anywhere else, just comprehend it in "I don't know." If you can penetrate these three words, the task of your whole life's study will be completed.

67 Where to Escape

Our great Buddhist sages could empty out all characteristics and achieve knowledge of the myriad things, but even they could not instantly obliterate what was fixed by their actions, so how could commonplace ordinary people? Since you are one of them, layman, I think you too should enter this state of concentration (I'm about to indicate). In times past there was a monk who asked an old adept, "The world is so hot, I don't know where to go to escape." The old adept said, "Escape into a boiling cauldron, into the coals of a furnace." The monk said, "In a cauldron of boiling water or the coals of a furnace, how does one escape?" The adept said, "The multitude of sufferings cannot reach there." I hope that in the conduct of your daily activities you will meditate just like this. The advice of old adepts shouldn't be neglected.

This is my own prescription for getting results. I wouldn't consent to pass it on to you freely unless this Path accorded with you and you were acquainted with this Mind. It just takes a moment when the accord (with the Path) is crude: being in the boiling water, you don't need to use any other boiling water. If he uses some other boiling water, this makes the person go mad. You must realize this. One moment when the accord is crude—don't look elsewhere, just in your daily activities and conduct as a layman. Where bright, it's as bright as the sun; where dark, it's as dark as lacquer. If wherever you pick it up, you reflect on it uniformly with the light of the fundamental ground, there's no going wrong: you can kill people and you can bring people to life. Therefore the buddhas and ancestral teachers have always gone into the boiling cauldron, into the coals of the furnace, using this medicine to cure birth and death, the great disease that afflicts sentient beings with suffering. They are called the Great Kings of Physicians. I don't know whether you believe fully or not, layman. If you say you possess a secret method not handed down from father to son, a subtle technique that doesn't use going into the boiling cauldron, into the coals of a furnace to escape, then I hope you'll bestow it on me.

68 Excerpts from Instructions Given in the Master's Room

I wait for people who are intent and sincere: it takes people whose qualities are right. This is directly entering the stage of Tathagata with a single leap: studying Ch'an requires a straightforward mind and straightforward conduct, direct words and direct speech. Since mind and words are straightforward and direct, from beginning to end, through all the stages, there will never be all the petty detailed aspects within them. The Ancestral Teacher came from the West, directly pointing to the human mind, (letting people) see their inherent nature and achieve buddhahood. A monk asked Yun Men, "What is Buddha?" Yun Men said, "A dry piece of shit." If you try to think it over, you've already distorted it and even made it untrue.

These days the brethren have much knowledge and emotional understanding—they have to come here to answer with idle words and long-winded talk. It's as if you held a priceless wish-fulfilling gem in the palm of your hand, but when asked by someone "What's that in your hand?" you put down the gem and pick up a clump of dirt. How stupid! If you go on this way, even if you study until the (nonexistent) Year of the Ass, you won't awaken.

Here at my place there's no doctrine to be given to people: I just wrap up the case on the basis of the facts. It's just as if you bring a crystal pitcher which you cherish like anything, and as soon as I see it, I smash it for you. And if you bring a wish-fulfilling gem, I'll take it away from you. Seeing you come this way, I'll cut off your two hands for you.

Therefore Master Lin Chi, said, "When I meet a Buddha, I slay the Buddha; when I meet an Ancestral Teacher, I slay the Ancestral Teacher; when I meet an Arhat,* I slay the Arhat."

---

* An Arhat is one who has conquered the afflictions of passion and put an end to the attachments of greed, wrath, and ignorance.

But say, since Lin Chi is called a spiritual friend, a man of knowledge, why then does he kill people? Look and see what principle of his this is. Where is the mistake of the brethren these days who do not realize this as they do their meditation? It's just their wanting to understand him. As for "This way won't do, and not this way won't do either: so or not so, neither will do"—what is right? Can you use a turning word to understand? If you can't understand him, then the man of old was too concise and direct. But you don't consent to go to where he was concise and direct to act: it's just because it's so perfectly clear that it makes your attainment slow.

69 Open Talk at the Invitation of Ch'ien Chi-yi

The Dharma cannot be seen, heard, perceived, or known. If you employ seeing, hearing, perception, or knowing, then this is seeing, hearing, perception, or knowing—it's not seeking the Dharma. Since it's outside of seeing, hearing, perception, and knowing, what then will you call "the Dharma"? When you get here, it's like a man drinking water—he knows for himself whether it is cold or warm. Only if you personally witness it and awaken to it can you see the Dharma. For a person who has really witnessed and awakened, when a single hair is picked up, he at once can understand the whole great earth.

These days not only Ch'an people but even gentlemen of affairs, intelligent, quick-witted, deeply learned men, all have two diseases. Not to pay attention, not to attach the mind (to things)—this is "forgetting concerns." When they forget concerns, they tumble down beneath the black mountain (of oblivion), into the ghost cave. In the Teachings they call it "dark torpor." When they do pay attention and attach the mind (to things), the mind's discriminating consciousness flies around in confusion, one thought after another, the next thought continuing even before the previous thought has ended. In the Teachings they call this "excitation." (People caught in torpor/excitation) do not realize that right where each and every person is, is One Great Matter that's neither sunk in torpor nor roused in excitation, like the universal cover of the sky, like the universal support of the earth. This Great Matter existed before there was a world, and when the world is destroyed, this Great Matter won't stir a hairsbreadth.

Usually gentlemen of affairs are roused in excitation, so these days in all localities there's a certain perverted "silent illumination" Ch'an: seeing that gentlemen of affairs are obstructed by sensory afflictions, so their hearts are not at peace, they teach them to be "cold ashes, a dead tree," or "a single strip of bleached white cloth," or "an incense brazier in an ancient shrine," to act sad and coldly indifferent. But tell me, the man who takes this rest—can he rest too? They don't realize at all: how can you rest if this monkey isn't dead? How can you rest if the one that comes as the vanguard and leaves as the rearguard isn't dead?

Last year on the road to Fukien, this ("silent illumination" teaching) style was extremely prevalent. When I went to Fukien in the 1130s to dwell (alone) in a hut, I tried to dispel it, saying it cuts off enlightenment's life of wisdom, saying that even if a thousand Buddhas appeared in the world, (the "silent illumination" people) wouldn't know repentance. Among them there was the gentleman Cheng Shang-ming. Being very intelligent, he could understand rationally the Buddhist Teachings and the Taoist Canon, and Confucianism of course. One day he came to my room holding a stick of incense. His anger was palpable, his tone and demeanor stern. He said, "I have a stick of incense not yet burned: I want to get a certain matter understood with you. You have freely denounced (the idea that) wordless silence is the highest resting place among the Dharma's methods. I suspect you are unable to believe this because you have never reached this stage. What about Old Shakyamuni closing his door and not making a sound for twenty-one days back in Magadha—wasn't this the silence of a Buddha? When the thirty-two bodhisattvas each expounded the Dharma-gate of Nonduality, and at the end (when it came his turn) Vimalakirti had no words to say and Manjusri praised him—wasn't this the silence of bodhisattvas? When Subhuti was sitting quietly on the cliff, wordless, without speaking—wasn't this the silence of a shravaka? When Indra saw Subhuti sitting quietly on the cliff and so showered down flowers as an offering, also without speaking—wasn't this the silence of an ordinary being? When Bodhidharma went from Liang to Wei and sat impassively for nine years—wasn't this the silence of an ancestral teacher? As soon as Lu Tsu saw a monk, he would face the wall—wasn't this the silence of a teacher of the Ch'an School? Why then do you struggle to displace 'silent illumination' and consider it false and wrong?"

I said, Shang-ming, it's good you asked; now wait while I tell you. If I can't explain satisfactorily, then I'll burn the incense and pay homage to you with three bows. If I can explain, then I'll accept your respects.

I'm not going to talk to you about old Shakyamuni or the sayings of the past worthies (of Ch'an). I'm going to go right into your house to explain—as it's called, borrowing an old lady's shawl to visit an old lady. So I'll ask you, Have you ever read Chuang Tzu?

"Of course."

Chuang Tzu said, "Neither words nor silence are sufficient to convey the ultimate of the Tao or of things: their meaning culminates in neither words nor silence." I haven't read Kuo Hsiang's (standard) commentary or the explanations of the various schools—I'm just going by my own interpretation to refute this silence of yours. In essence the ultimate of the Tao and of things lies neither in speech nor in silence—words cannot convey it, nor can silence. So what you've said doesn't even accord with Chuang Tzu's meaning—how could you be in accord with the intent of great teachers like old Shakyamuni and Bodhidharma?

Do you want to know the meaning of Chuang Tzu's "Their meaning culminates in neither speech nor silence"? It's this: The Great Master Yun Men lifted up a fan and said, "This fan leaps up into the thirty-third heaven and taps on Indra's nostrils. One blow to a carp in the Eastern Sea, and the rain pours down."

If you can understand, these words that Yun Men said are the same as what Chuang Tzu said.

At this point he didn't make a sound; I said to him, Though you don't speak, in your heart you still haven't submitted. Nevertheless, the men of old definitely didn't understand by sitting. You just brought up Shakyamuni closing his door and Vimalakirti's silence. Well, look at this: In olden times there was a lecturer called Dharma Master Chao, who explained that wordlessness to people saying, "Shakyamuni closing his door in Magadha, Vimalakirti keeping his mouth shut at Vaisali, Subhuti chanting without speaking to reveal the Path, and Indra without hearing showering down flowers—all these are to be understood as spiritual visitations. Thus when the mouth takes them up it falls silent. How could one say they had no discernment? Actually, they discerned what cannot be said." When this truth suddenly collides with one's spirit, and he arrives unawares where speaking is impossible, though he doesn't speak, his voice is like thunder. That's why Seng Chao said, "How could one say they had no discernment, since they discerned what cannot be said?"

Here, worldly intelligence and talents cannot be used at all. When you reach such a stage, this at last is the place to abandon your body and your life. This kind of realm requires each person to experience and awaken for himself. Therefore the Hua Yen Scripture says, "The Tathagata's palace is boundless: naturally those who awaken are within it." This is the gate of great liberation of all the sages since antiquity, boundless and immeasurable, without gain or loss, without silence or speech, without going or coming: So in every atom of dust, So in every land, So in every moment, So in every phenomenon.

Since the capacity of sentient beings is (often) narrow and meager, they don't get to the realms of the sages of the Three Teachings. Therefore they distinguish this and that: far from knowing that the world is this vast, instead they go sit in silence under the black mountain, inside the ghost cave. Thus the former sages decried this as the deep pit of liberation, a place to be feared. Seen with the eye of penetrating spiritual powers, it's the same as sitting on a mountain of knives or in a forest of swords, in a boiling cauldron or in the coals of a furnace. If lecturers don't even get stuck in silence, how can members of the School of the Ancestral Teachers? If you say, "As soon as you open your mouth, you fall," right now, this has nothing to do with it.

Shang-ming bowed without realizing it. I said, Though you bow, there's still something the matter: Come to my room tonight. (When he came) I asked how old he was this year. He said sixty-four. Again I asked, Where did you come from sixty-four years ago? He couldn't open his mouth, and I drove him out with blows across the back with a bamboo rod. The next day he came to my room again and said, "Sixty-four years ago I didn't even exist—how then can you ask me where I came from?" I said, Sixty-four years ago, you couldn't have always been in the Cheng family. This one perfectly clear solitary light, listening to and expounding the Dharma right now—

ultimately, where was it before you were born? He said, "I don't know." I said, If you don't know, then birth is a big thing. But this life is limited to a hundred years. Until you fly beyond the cosmos, you'll have to go into the coffin with it. At that time, as the four elements and five *skandhas* all at once disperse, though you have eyes you don't see things, though you have ears you don't hear sounds, though your heart is there as a lump of flesh discrimination doesn't operate, though you have a body you can be burned with fire or cut with knives without feeling pain. When you get here, after all, where does the clear solitary light go to? He said, "I don't know that either." I said, If you don't know, then death is a big thing. Thus it's said, "Impermanence is swift, the matter of birth and death is great"—it's the same principle. Here, intelligence cannot be used, nor memories held. Again I'll ask you: Your whole life you've made up so many little word games, when the last day of your life arrives, which phrase are you going to use to oppose birth and death? To succeed you must know clearly where we come from at birth and where we go at death. If you don't know, you're a fool. At last his heart submitted. After this I taught him not to sit in wordlessness, and he agreed to come here to meditate.

To Tseng T'ien-yu

70 "Silent Illumination"

Old P'ang said, "Just resolve to empty all that exists: don't make real all that doesn't exist." Just master these two propositions, and your whole life's task of study is completed.

These days there's a breed of shaven-headed outsiders

whose own eyes are not clear, who just teach people to stop and rest and play dead. Even if you stop and rest like this until a thousand buddhas appear in the world, you still won't be able to stop and rest—you'll be making your mind even more confused and troubled. They teach people to "keep the mind still," to "forget feelings" according to circumstances, to practice "silent illumination." As they go on and on "illuminating" and "keeping the mind still," they add to their confusion and oppression, with no end to it. Utterly losing the expedient means of the ancestral teachers, they instruct others wrongly, teaching people to go on in vain and wastefully with birth and death; furthermore, they teach people not to care about this state of affairs. "Simply go on putting things to rest this way," they'll say. "When you've stopped feelings as they come and thoughts are not produced, at such a time it's not unknowing silence—in fact, it's alert and awake and perfectly clear." This kind is even more pernicious, blinding people's eyes.

To have people "keep the mind still"—this is an interpretation produced by holding to the awareness before one's eyes. To have people rigidly "stop and rest"—this is an interpretation produced by holding to the empty stillness of forgetting concerns. To say that when one has put things to rest to the point that he is unawares and unknowing, like earth, wood, tile, or stone, this is not unknowing silence—this is a view born of wrongly taking too literally words that were (only) expedient means to free bonds. To teach people to reflect according to circumstances and take care not to let any bad perceptions appear—this again is an interpretation produced by accepting the skull's emotional consciousness. To teach people just to be expansive and give free rein to their mastery, not to be concerned if mind is born or thoughts stir, since fundamentally there's no real essence to the creation and destruction of thoughts, and if one holds to them as real the mind of birth and death is born—this again is an interpretation produced by holding to the natural body as the ultimate thing.

All the above diseases are not the students' doings—they're all due to the wrong instructions of blind teachers.

To Chang An-kuo

71   Enlightenment the Key

Some take sitting wordlessly with eyes shut beneath the black mountain, inside the ghost cave, and consider it as the scene on the Other Side of the Primordial Buddha, the scene before their parents were born—they also call it "silent yet ever illuminating," and consider it Ch'an. This lot don't seek subtle wondrous enlightenment: they consider enlightenment as falling into the secondary. They think that enlightenment deceives people, that enlightenment is a fabrication. Since they've never awakened themselves, they don't believe anyone has awakened. As I once told some monks, without enlightenment, you cannot even get the wondrous subtlety of worldly arts and techniques, much less escape from birth and death.

There's a kind acting as teachers spreading false talk who tell students, "Just preserve stillness." (Asked,) "What thing is this, preserving? Who is the still one?" they say "The still one is the basis." Yet they don't believe that the enlightened one exists: they say that the enlightened one is an offshoot, and quote this from Yang Shan: A monk asked Yang Shan, "Do people these days still make use of enlightenment or not?" Yang Shan said, "Though enlightenment is not absent, nevertheless it falls into the secondary: don't talk of dreams in front of fools." Then they understand this (literally) as a real doctrine, and say that enlightenment is secondary.

Such people scarcely realize that Kuei Shan himself had a saying to alert students; indeed, it's very cogent: "Enlightenment is the standard for investigating the ultimate truth through to the end." Where do (those false teachers) put these words? It's impossible that Kuei Shan was bringing doubts and error to later people by having them fall into the secondary.

(Kuei Shan was Yang Shan's teacher.)

72 A Talk to the Assembly

An ancient said, "Great Wisdom has no discrimination, Great Function has no principle or phenomena—like the moon leaving its image in a thousand rivers, like a wave following a multitude of streams."

But what is Great Wisdom without discrimination? What is Great Function without principle or phenomena? Isn't Great Wisdom "asked one, answering ten," "eloquence pouring out like a waterfall"? Isn't Great Wisdom things like "coarse words and subtle speech all returning to the supreme meaning," "overturning the meditation seat and scattering the congregation with shouts," and "hitting immediately when they hesitate in thought"? If you understand in this fashion, don't say you are a patchrobed monk—in the school of patchrobed monks, you are not even fit to be a servant who picks up the worn-out straw sandals and filthy bags. A spiritual friend with real experience and genuine awakening, but who doesn't understand the Great Dharma, can't avoid instructing people with his own realization and his own awakening when he helps them, and so he blinds his eyes. How much the more so do those without the experience of enlightenment, those who've learned the words, blind people's eyes—it goes without saying. This Matter is very difficult: even for immeasurably great people, when they get here, there's no place to join in. So how can a bunch of devils like you, with small faculties and no knowledge, dare to open your big mouths so carelessly?

Try to sit in a quiet place and investigate in detail: in your heart, have you really arrived at the stage where you don't doubt, or not? If you haven't really gotten there, but I nevertheless acknowledged that you are able to let go and hold fast, and are not subject to being bent out of shape by others, then this type (of "teaching") is called "the mire of hell."

Every grain of rice and stalk of vegetable brought by the donors of the ten directions to give to you, is just so that you will accomplish your work in the Path, and proceed together (with them) on the vehicle of enlightenment—they seek reward in future lives. If you do not accomplish your work in the Path, how can you consume (their offerings)?

If all of you people want to perpetuate the ways of this school, you must know the One Suchness of mind and objects: only then will you have a small share of realization. You shouldn't see me saying such things and then hide your eyes and act dead, forcibly arranging mind and objects in "one suchness." Even with all your abilities, how could you arrange for this? Do you want to attain true One Suchness of mind and objects? It requires an abrupt, complete break: pick out the one inside your skull that's doing the false thinking, take the eighth consciousness, and cut it off with one blow. Naturally you don't apply any arrangements.

Haven't you read Master Yen T'ou's saying? "As soon as there's something considered important, it becomes a nest." All of you people have spent your whole lives in Ch'an communities inquiring after This Matter—without any attainment, needless to say. Among you there are many with gray heads and yellow teeth, sitting in your nests your whole lives without being able to come out, totally unaware of your error. Those who've become infatuated with the words and phrases of the ancients take amazing words and subtle phrases as their nest. Those who take delight in the verbal meaning of the scriptures take the scriptures as their nest. Those infatuated with the nature of mind take "The triple world is only mind, the myriad phenomena only consciousness" as their nest. Those who've become infatuated with quiescent silence without words or speech take shutting their eyes, "the Other Side of the Primordial Buddha," sitting motionless under the black mountain, inside the ghost cave, as their nest. All the above have things they consider important where their infatuations lie. Lacking the qualities of great men of power to step back and recognize their error, they think of what they consider important as extraordinary, as wondrous and subtle, as peace and security, as the ultimate, as liberation. For those who entertain such thoughts, even if Buddha appeared in the world, it would be to no avail. In the Teachings they are called deluded, stupid, and confused. Why? Because you are deluded, stupid, and confused. Why? Because you are deluded, you cling to the false as if it were true. Because you are stupid, you fall down into what you consider important, and cannot move or turn. If there's nothing aroused in the mind and no attachment to phenomena, then there's nothing considered important. With nothing considered important, naturally you're full of rawboned power, without desire or dependence, and master of the Dharma.

So right now you want such realization. It's not hard, either: simply be equanimous in your mind, without any defiling attachments. What are defiling attachments? Thoughts of sentient beings and buddhas, thoughts of the world and leaving the world, thoughts of seeking detachment and enlightened knowledge—all these are called defiling attachments. Just boldly apply your spiritual energy before desire arises, and leap out with a single bound—This Mind will be shining bright, alone and liberated. The instant you awaken to this, turn above it: then naturally it will be clear everywhere and revealed in everything. And when you get to such a stage, you must not watch over it. If you watch over it, then there's something you consider important; as soon as there's something considered important, this mind leaks—then it's called the leaking mind, not the equanimous mind of even sameness. "Even sameness" means good and evil are equal, turning away and turning towards are equal, inner truth and outer events are equal, ordinary and sage are equal, finite and infinite are equal, essence and function are equal. This truth can only be known by those who experience it. All of you people who haven't yet experienced it simply must do so. Only when you've experienced it completely can you be called a true leaver of home. Those whose minds don't experience this, and who seek the experience outside of mind, are called homeleaving outsiders: they're not fit to plant weeds.

This Mind is broad and vast, without divisions, without sides or surface: all the buddhas, numerous as the sands, attaining true awakening, the mountains, rivers, and the great earth, the profuse array of myriad images—all are within This

Mind. This Mind can put names on everything, but nothing can put a name on it. Therefore all the buddhas and ancestral teachers could not but go along with your mistake and attach names to it, calling it True Suchness, Buddha-nature, Enlightenment and Nirvana, imposing all kinds of different appellations. Because in the world of you sentient beings, views are biased and insensitive, with all sorts of differentiation, they set up these different names to enable you, amidst differentiation, to recognize This Mind that has no difference—it's not that This Mind has differences.

Buddha said, "One may wish to reveal it with comparisons, but in the end there is no comparison that can explain this." Saying it's broad and vast has already limited it, to say nothing of wanting to enter this broad and vast realm with the limited mind. Even if you managed thereby to enter, it would be like taking a ladle to ladle out the ocean: though the ladle is filled, how much could it hold? Nevertheless, the water in the ladle, before it went in there, was identical to the limitless water (of the ocean). Likewise, because your world is just this big, and you feel satisfied with it, this limitless world adapts to your capacity and fills it up. It's not that the water of the great ocean is only this much. Therefore Buddha said, "It's like the great ocean, not deferring whether mosquitos or titans drink its water—all get their fill." Mosquitos and titans symbolize the difference between great and small: basically, in essence, This Mind doesn't have so many differences. Just don't create so many views, and recognize This Mind: then you'll be able to know all kinds of differences too.

The former sages didn't even hold to This Mind as real: outside of mind, what else is there real that can obstruct you? Today I have dragged through the mud and water—again, it's for lack of alternative. It's from old ladylike kindness, admonishing a beloved child, soothing a favorite son, that I've drawn out so many ramifications. Don't remember what I've said, and consider it right. Today I speak this way, but then tomorrow I'll speak otherwise. As soon as you're thus, I am not thus; when you're not thus, then I am thus. Where will you search out my abiding place? Since I myself don't even know, how can anyone else find where I stay?

This is the living gate: you can enter only when you've put to death your fabricated "reality."* Yet students these days consider a bit of zeal, paying homage to the Buddha, upholding the scriptures, and disciplining themselves in body, mouth, and mind, as their sustenance, hoping to find realization. What does this have to do with it? There are like fools intent on going west to get something in the east—the farther they go, the farther away they are; the greater the hurry, the greater the delay. This is the gate of the Great Dharma: unconditioned, undefiled, without accomplishment. If you arouse the slightest notion of gaining experience of it, you are running off in the opposite direction. How can you hope for it, wanting to rely on some petty, contrived accomplishments?

Here at my place it's oyster-Ch'an: as soon as he opens his "mouth," you see his guts—the unusual jewels and unique gems are all right there. But when he keeps his "mouth" shut, where can you find his crack?

It's not a forced action: the Dharma is fundamentally like this. All of you should value the time, and each and every one take advantage of his physical vigor (while it lasts) to exert his spirit and comprehend (the Dharma) completely. Don't take a liking to other people's marvels—the marvelous misleads people. If the various poisons are in your mind and consciousness, don't say you've gained power: another day, when you're dying,

---

* According to Buddhism what we customarily perceive as the world of outer objects and inner self is but the manifestation of force of habit, of seeds within the storehouse consciousness reified through our acts within a set of causes and conditions.

you won't attain instantaneous liberation as you die—how can you go on talking of being a match for birth and death?

The afflictions of worldly ignorance all are limited. The moment you see through them, they are quiescent and extinct in their very essence. The afflictions of evil knowledge and evil views, of (attachment to) the "dust of the Dharma," are limitless. They can obstruct your eye for the Path, and cause your mind and consciousness to slander the Buddha, Dharma, and Sangha day and night, creating hellish karma. Though it's a good thing, it's turned around to bring on a bad result. Only great men of power, possessed of wisdom, can see through (the Dharma) and not be afflicted by it.

Haven't you read the saying of the Great Master Yun Men? "Take the whole universe at once and put it on your eyelashes." As all of you people listen to such talk, I don't dare hope that you will come forth boldly and give me a punch! So let's investigate it slowly and thoroughly: is it existent or nonexistent? What principle is this? Even if you could understand here, in the school of patchrobed monks, you should have your feet broken. If you were a man (a real Ch'an man), when you heard me say, "Where are there old adepts appearing in the world?" you should have spit right in my face. If you don't act this way, but accept things as soon as you hear someone bring them up, you've already fallen into the secondary.

Again, haven't you seen Master Lo Shan's saying? "The mystic gate has no doctrines, establishes no general principles. If you want to search for it, look before the sound." All you disciples of Buddha, real mind is not fixed, and real wisdom is not bounded. Even if I let these two lips go on talking from now till the end of time without a break, you still can't depend on another person's power: this is a matter in which each and every person is fully sufficient in his own right. It can neither be augmented nor diminished the least little bit. The buddhas and ancestral teachers attain it, and it's called the Dharma Gate of Great Liberation. Sentient beings lose it, and it's called the affliction of sensory troubles. Though attained, still it's never attained; though lost, still it's never lost. Gain and loss pertain to the people, not to the Dharma.

Therefore the Third Ancestral Teacher said:

The Ultimate Path has no difficulties—
Just avoid picking and choosing.
Don't hate or love
And be lucid and clear.
When there's the slightest distinction
It's as far apart as heaven and earth.
If you want it to appear before you,
Don't keep to going with and going against.

Each of you followers of Ch'an should think back: have you ever put your mind to this and understood it? The Ancestral Teacher gave it a name, calling it "The Inscription of the Mind of Faith." He just wanted everyone to believe that this broad and vast wondrous mind of quiescent extinction is definitely not attained from other people. Thus in it he said:

If the one mind isn't born,
The myriad phenomena are without fault.
No fault, no phenomena,
Not born, not mind.
Subject is extinguished along with objects;
Objects are submerged along with subject.
Objects are objects because of subjects;
Subjects are subjects because of objects.

He also said, "The Great Path, its body is broad: without ease, without difficulty." And he also said:

Hold to it and you lose it,
And are bound to enter false roads.

Let go of it and naturally
Its essence has no going or staying.

Just have faith in this Truth of One Mind: it cannot be grasped,
it cannot be rejected. Then you should give up your body and
your life right there. If you cannot give them up, it's because
of your own hesitancy—on the last day of your life, don't
blame me.

The weather is hot and you've been standing a long time.

Ta Hui gave a shout and descended from the seat.

Lineage and Names

Ta Hui is reckoned as belonging to the sixteenth generation of Ch'an down from the Six Ancestral Teacher Hui Neng. The lineage runs: Hui Neng—Nan Yueh Huai Jang—Ma Tsu Tao Yi—Pai Chang Huai Hai—Huang Po Hsi Yun—Lin Chi I Hsuan—Hsing Hua Ts'un Chiang—Nan Yan Hui Yung—Feng Hsueh T'ing Chao—Shou Shan Hsing Nien—Fen Yang Shan Chao—Shih Shuang Chu Yuan—Yang Chi Fang Hui—Pai Yun Shou Tuan—Wu Tsu Fa Yen—Yuan Wu K'e Ch'in—Ta Hui Tsung Kao.

At the time *Swampland Flowers* was first published, the Wade-Giles transliteration of Chinese was still in use in the English-speaking world; by now this has been superseded by the Pinyin transliteration system used in the People's Republic of China.

For reference, here is a chart giving the names mentioned in *Swampland Flowers* in the Wade-Giles version as in the translation text, along with the Pinyin equivalents, and the Japanese readings of the Chinese names.

Lineage and Names

WADE-GILES VERSION	PINYIN VERSION	JAPANESE READING
Lin Chi Ch'an	Linji Chan	Rinzai Zen
Ts'ao Tung Ch'an	Caodong Chan	Sōtō Zen
kung an	gongan	kōan
Ta Hui Tung Kao	Dahui Zonggao	Daie
Yuan Wu	Yuanwu	Engo
Ch'ang Ch'ing	Chang Qing	Chōkei
Chao Chou	Zhaozhou	Jōshū
Hsueh Feng	Xuefeng	Seppō
Hui Neng	Huineng	Enō
Kuei Shan	Guishan	Isan
Hung Chih	Hongzhi	Wanshi
Wu Tsu Fa Yen	Wuzu Fayan	Goso Hōen
Ch'ang Sha	Changsha	Chōsha
Great Being Fu	Great Being Fu	Fu Daishi
Hsueh T'ou	Xuetou	Setchō
Jui Yen	Ruiyan	Zuigan
Kuei Tsung	Guizong	Kisu
Lin Chi	Linji	Rinzai
Ma Tsu	Mazu	Baso
Nan Ch'uan	Nanquan	Nansen
Layman P'ang	Laymen Pang	Bō
Te Shan	Deshan	Tokusan
Tu Shun	Dushun	Tojun
Yun Men	Yunmen	Ummon
Lo Shan	Luoshan	Rasan
Mu Chou	Muzhou	Bakushū

WADE-GILES VERSION	PINYIN VERSION	JAPANESE READING
P'an Shan	Panshan	Banzan
Seng Ch'ao	Sengzhao	Sōjō
T'ou Tzu	Touzi	Tōsu
Yen T'ou	Yantou	Gantō
Yung Chia	Yongjia	Yōka

Printed in the United States
by Baker & Taylor Publisher Services